THESE STONES · TV SERIES
OFFICIAL STUDY GUIDE

Your Personal Devotional &
Group Handbook for Season 1

CHERYL MCKAY
SUSAN ROHRER

STONE IMPACT
MEDIA

THESE STONES
YOUR PERSONAL DEVOTIONAL &
GROUP HANDBOOK FOR SEASON 1
THESE STONES: TV SERIES
OFFICIAL STUDY GUIDE

Written by Cheryl McKay & Susan Rohrer

Readers may reach out to authors via:
www. purplepenworks.com (Cheryl)
facebook.com/SusanRohrerAuthor

Kindly direct professional inquiries to:
cheryl@stoneimpactmedia.com

Follow the TV series *These Stones* at:
https://www.facebook.com/thesestones

Stream *These Stones* TV Series episodes at:
https://upfaithandfamily.com/thesestones

Quotations from our *These Stones* cast and crew members mentioned by real names in this book have been drawn and edited from Behind-the-Scenes promotional interviews and as such include voluntary statements contributed (per written agreement upon hire) to support on-going promotion and distribution efforts for the TV series *These Stones* in any and all media. Said media is deemed to include this book publication in any and all formats as well as all other forms of promotion designed to support, engage, and enhance viewers' experience of *These Stones* as a television series.

True story anecdotes with real names are used by permission and with gratitude.

While Scripture text bracketed [as such] varies from the wording of the New American Standard Bible®, all bracketed words are alternate translations of the Greek or Hebrew and consistent with the meaning of the respective original languages of the Bible. This includes instances where the Bible's original language/s, such as the Greek *anthropos* or gender-based pronouns reference all people.

Cover image:
©2024 THESE STONES – Season 1
Series Screenshot: Farm Property Aerial
From the award-winning drone photography of *These Stones* 2nd Unit Director and Editor, Judd Brannon

Cheryl McKay Author Photo:
By Vincent Wallace

Susan Rohrer Author Photo:
By Adam DeBenedittis

ISBN-13: 979-8-9912519-0-7 (Paperback)

ISBN 13: 979-8-9912519-1-4 (Hardcover)

1   2   3   4   5   6   7   8   9   10   11   12

McKay, Cheryl
Rohrer, Susan

These Stones
Your Personal Devotional &
Group Handbook for Season 1
These Stones: TV Series
Official Study Guide

Published by Stone Impact Media

Published in the United States of America
for Worldwide Distribution

First Edition 2024

To the living stones in the household of faith.
May you have eyes to see and ears to hear
God's messages of faith, hope, and love.

When your children ask their fathers in time to come, saying, "What are these stones?" then you shall inform your children…

—Joshua 4:21–22a

CONTENTS

FROM SUSAN

THESE STONES Roadmap

plan

---

*"For I know the plans that I have for you," declares the
LORD, "plans for welfare and not calamity to give you a
future and a hope."*

—Jeremiah 29:11

Embarking on this kind of study can be a unique journey.
In a way, it's like life in the Spirit. You never know
exactly what will happen along the way. But you step into the
future God gives to you with hope.

Sometimes you're called to go out on your own with
your heavenly Father. Other times, you might travel along
with family or friends. Jesus did both. So whether you're with
earthly or divine companionship as you venture through this
study—it's all good.

Want to know where we're headed? What follows is a
quick peek for you.

Your Itinerary

Before we set off, here are some travel tips to get the most out of Season One and this Study Guide.

1. **PLAN**: Schedule regular time to watch each *These Stones* television episode solo—or if you're in a group, plan a time to huddle with any study buddies after viewing each episode.

2. **WATCH**: Watch each 30–35-minute episode in sequence.

3. **READ:** If you're studying in a group, read through the corresponding episode's chapter in advance of meeting. Solo or group travelers: keep your spiritual eyes and ears open as you read. Note anything God may impress upon you. (Any message that's truly from God will be in perfect alignment with the full counsel of the Holy Bible.)

4. **GATHER**: Get together with any study buddies. If you're flying solo, invite the Holy Spirit to partner with you along the way. Acknowledge God's presence to guide.

5. **APPLY**: Answer the *Discussion Questions* that follow the body of each chapter. We'll leave plenty of space for paperback and hardcover users to journal answers. Our eBook readers may opt to use a blank journal or notebook. Either way, you'll be able to apply what you've learned.

6. **PRAY**: Thank God for being your ever-present Teacher and Guide. You can pray along with the written prayers

we've provided at the end of each chapter and/or launch right into individual or group intercession.

7. **VENTURE**: Put your living and active faith into practice. Draw from the episode-specific *Activations* list at the end of each chapter.

Want More?

Check out the Bonus Content we've prepared for you toward the back of this book.

BONUS INTERVIEWS

Of course, you'll be hearing a lot from Cheryl McKay and me (Susan) as the authors of this book. (We've labeled our chapters, so you'll always know who's speaking.) Cheryl served as showrunner, creator, EP, and producer of our TV Series *These Stones,* while I served as first season director, co-EP, and wrote with Cheryl on our writing staff.

That said, we dearly love the whole team—cast and crew—that helped us bring *These Stones* to life. And we hope you'll be blessed to hear many of the insights some of our team members have expressed. (You'll also see a quote or two in each episode's chapter.)

But don't miss out on all the additional interviews we've included, right after our *Episode 1.6* chapter. There, you can explore many thoughts related by other members of our *These Stones* family.

We're a chatty bunch, so even after editing for length, it's still a chunky section, chock full of meaningful insights. Pull up a chair and get to know some of our team through their candid, unscripted responses to our questions.

BONUS ACTIVATIONS

Can't get enough of venturing out in the Spirit? Cheryl compiled a great list of additional ideas inspired by our series. What can I say? The woman is endlessly creative!

If you're a creative too, reading Cheryl's *Bonus Activations* list may spark even more ideas for you. It seems there are limitless ways you can go out into the world and share the love God gives us.

We'd love to hear your *Activations* experiences, so chime in on any of our official *These Stones* social media pages like: facebook.com/thesestones.

What's What?

These Stones will prompt more questions than it will reveal answers at first. It's a reflection of the mysterious ways God moves in our lives. Still, we figured a handful of series terms might help orient you to what's what along the way.

Couriers: people from Bible days on Appointment

Appointment: an assignment to help present-day people

Aides: present-day people who assist Couriers

Contemporaries: present-day people in need of help

Central Dispatch: where Appointments are set

The Corridor: a hall where Aides find Couriers

That's all we'll tip for you now—except our tagline. It's a biblical promise that's hidden in plain sight.

You Are Never Alone

As you watch *These Stones*, there's one line you'll hear in every episode. In one form or another, you'll hear someone tell someone else they're not alone. It's there to remind all of us, no matter what, of the promise of Jesus.

> *…and lo, I am with you always, even to the end of the age.*
> —Matthew 28:20

In celebration of God's goodness, the makers of *These Stones* invite you into the fellowship of our show and the adventure of this first season's study guide.

It's our hope that you'll sense His presence every step of the way. No matter if you watch or study individually, with someone else, or as part of a small group, know this:

The Lover of Your Soul is with you.

And He's the greatest Travel Guide of all.

Wonderful Father, thank You for the adventure You have prepared for me. I'm so grateful for the future and the hope You promise me in Christ. Quiet my heart to hear Your still, small voice as we travel through this study together.

How Stones Can Speak

See with your eyes, hear with your ears, and give attention to all that I am going to show you; for you have been brought here in order to show it to you...

—Ezekiel 40:4

Have you ever received a word from God, just when you needed it most? Have you seen something the Lord has been trying to show you?

Maybe a certain verse or someone's story from Bible days practically leapt off the pages of Scripture for you—resonating with present relevance. The Spirit could have spoken words of comfort or encouragement through another person, just when you needed it. He may have used a faith-based book, film, or artwork to speak into your life.

Perhaps the Lord showed you some kind of signpost or symbolic object that engaged you to mine out its deeper meaning. Maybe that divine dispatch came as a single, Spirit-breathed word on a stone.

If that's you, you know what receiving even one word on a stone from God can be like. You know what a gem these messages can be. They're a literal Godsend. They remind us how He was there for us in that moment. They reinforce that divine interaction and the truth of His life-giving words.

Memory-Jogging Stones

You may have noticed that there's quite a bit of stone imagery in the Bible. Have you seen where stones were used to prompt people to retell the stories of what God had done?

I don't know about you, but I need reminders.

So did the children of Israel.

After leading God's people through the parted waters of the Jordan, Joshua told the heads of each tribe to carry stones from the middle of the river to serve as a memorial. That way, if the parents forgot how God brought them there, those river-smoothed stones would be there to catch their children's eyes.

> *This shall be a sign among you...* 21 *And [Joshua] said to the sons of Israel, "When your children ask their fathers in time to come, saying, "What are these stones?" 22 then you shall inform your children, saying, "Israel crossed this Jordan on dry ground.*
>
> —Joshua 4:6a, 21–22

Their kids and their kid's kids would come to ask that same question: *"What are these stones?"*

Of course, there was no power in the stones themselves (or in any created object). The Ten Commandments had already made it clear that they shouldn't be worshipped. The stones were just inanimate objects God used to remind them of His presence and what He'd said or done. In turn, the story would inform future generations.

In our television series *These Stones*, it's kind of like the way McKenna couldn't stop wondering about all the stones her mother left behind. How did these stones connect with everything her mom tried to tell her about her vibrant faith and how the Bible came to life for her?

Curiosity drew McKenna to mull over the same question we see in verse 21.

"What do these stones mean?"

Those questions engaged McKenna to find out how that pile of stones came to her late mother. They compelled her to start digging for answers. What really happened? Could her mom's claim be more than a delusion? Did a supernatural door really open when she read those Bibles in her prayer closet?

How About You?

Take a moment to ask yourself:

- In what ways does God speak to me?
- Can I recall a time when I recognized His voice?
- Do I relate to the people I read about in the Bible, in ways that help me with my life?

Understanding Our Allegory

You'll notice a paragraph at the beginning of each episode saying that *These Stones* includes people from Bible days. Here's the text of that paragraph:

This contemporary series explores a premise and characters from biblical history. Fictionalized elements are allegorical, designed to honor the truth.

Like the figurative parables Jesus told, lengthier allegories are created stories. They're imbedded with symbolic meaning. Parables and allegories alike can be infused with Kingdom truth for those who have eyes to see and ears to hear. Characters can represent something beyond themselves, in ways that are universal to the human condition.

These Stones uses an amazing New Testament passage as the springboard for our allegory. Picture the scene unfolding.

And Jesus cried out again with a loud voice, and gave up His spirit. 51 *And behold, the veil of the temple was torn in two from top to bottom; and the earth shook and the rocks were split.* 52 *The tombs were opened, and many bodies of the saints who had fallen asleep were raised;* 53 *and coming out of the tombs after His resurrection, they entered the holy city and appeared to many.*

—Matthew 27:50–53

Wait... What?

Yes. You read that right. After Jesus died and was raised from the dead, many saints who had died before Him were also brought back to life.

But these resurrected Bible people didn't just pop in and pop out unnoticed. They went into Jerusalem. What's more, they started appearing to many people in the city.

To be crystal clear—the Bible isn't talking about anything that has to do with ghosts or reincarnation. And neither are we. Nobody came back as something or someone else. Nobody's seeing dead people here.

Rather, the Bible says that these human saints were raised—as in from death to life. That means any godly person who died before Jesus could have been raised after He was. And those resurrected saints headed into the city. They started to interact with other living people.

What was next? Well, the Scriptures are silent about what happened to those risen saints after verse 53. The Bible doesn't tell us if they went on living and appearing to people or if they eventually died again. We simply don't know.

But that's where our fictional allegory kicks in.

Picture how this miraculous, biblical scenario could have unfolded *if* those saints had only been appointed to die once, as Scripture says we are. Envision how that could have played out *if* they'd lived on and kept appearing to people—even to this day.

Know this: *These Stones* isn't taking a theological stance on what happened to those raised saints. We don't know if they later died again or lived on in some way. We're not taking a position on how Moses (who died) and Elijah (who didn't) appeared to Jesus at the transfiguration either.

These remain among Scripture's mysteries.

The appearances of biblical characters in *These Stones* aren't meant to be taken literally. They're meant to represent how living and active the Scriptures are and can be to each reader. Figuratively, they're meant to bring the people of the Bible and their stories to life in a way that's relevant to viewers like you.

You know how it goes. You might be reading someone's story in the Bible. And suddenly it's as if that person comes alive to you (figuratively). Or the Holy Spirit uses the experiences of those scriptural saints to speak into your life today.

These Stones is meant to draw us into experiencing God through His Word in that interactive way. Think about it.

- What if our quiet times weren't so quiet?
- What if God used the Bible and its people to speak into our lives today?

One of our lead actresses had this to say about how the modern-day application of Bible stories helps us.

"Sometimes when people are reading the Bible, they can't understand—or it's not speaking to them. And so, this is just a way to really get to know these stories, these characters, these values, and in a way that we can relate to in our personal lives."

—Charlene Amoia (Eliana)

Stories of people of faith help us relate to others, the same way our Couriers do in *These Stones*. It's not that they quote "chapter and verse" at us. Instead, they set a winsome example. Just as people in the Bible used to speak in the common language of their Bible days, they communicate with today's people in ways that today's people can understand.

Our Couriers stay consistent with the message of the Bible—including that they're still as fallible as the rest of us.

Oh, the Humanity

One reason I relate so strongly to the people of the Bible is their utter humanity. Even our heroes of the faith, like Elijah. This verse is a good reminder of that for me.

Elijah was a man with a nature like ours…

—James 5:17a

Sure, the saints of old tried to follow God. But they messed up at times. Like we do. Yet time and again, God forgave. Lovingly, He set His people back on course to resume the high callings on their lives.

That's why *These Stones* takes these resurrected saints off the pedestals people tend to erect for them. This show depicts them as the Bible depicts them—as flawed human beings, navigating a fallen world. Wisdom gleaned from past mistakes helps them relate to present-day people's struggles.

We may hope and pray that God will make things go perfectly for us. But just as the people in the Bible faced challenges, setbacks, and obstacles, so will our characters.

And so will we.

These Stones producer/actress Erin Bethea put it this way:

"We live in a broken world. And He lets that brokenness exist. Because that's what we chose. No, no. He's not a fairy godmother. Because we wouldn't be aware of our need for salvation if none of our problems existed."

—Erin Bethea (Drea/Ep 1.3)

That broken world is on full display for us in the Bible. God's Word gives us all the wisdom we need to navigate it. And the people of the Bible give us the chance to experience God speaking to us today—as often as we read.

At its heart, *These Stones* is a TV series about living in interactive relationship with God—and one another. It's about fulfilling what Jesus called the greatest commandments: to love God and love one another as we love ourselves (Matthew 22:36–40). It's about helping others and reminding them He's with them, speaking into their lives too.

How About You?

Reading the Bible interactively with the Holy Spirit is one of the most frequent ways God speaks into our lives. With that in mind, think about this.

- Are there certain people in the Bible you relate to or identify with when you read their stories? If so, write down that person's name. (We'll give you a chance to share about this connection you feel later.)

- Do you have a favorite among the parables of Jesus? Which character do you relate to?

One of my favorites is the parable of the lost sheep. That symbolic story has applications to every story and character in *These Stones*. I love the way our Great Shepherd never loses sight of us, no matter how far we may wander or lose our way. I adore Jesus for pursuing us with His love, then how He tenderly picks us up and brings us home. He welcomes us back into loving fellowship with Him and one another.

Living Stones

There's a treasure trove of meaningful stone imagery in Scripture. Yet perhaps one passage speaks most vividly to how God sees all those who follow Jesus.

> *And coming to Him as a living stone which has been rejected by men, but is choice and precious in the sight of God, 5 you also, as living stones, are being built up as a spiritual house for a holy priesthood, to offer up spiritual sacrifices acceptable to God through Jesus Christ.*
>
> —1 Peter 2:4–5

Think of yourself as one of those living stones. For a moment, picture yourself as one of many stones, built up into that spiritual house.

Got that picture?

- Describe your stone and where you see yourself.

Maybe you saw yourself something like I did. I pictured an ordinary, matte gray stone. It was kind of like the stones in our stories—except it was plain. I didn't see my stone with a word engraved on it.

Now, ask God to show you how He sees you.

A different picture may emerge.

You could look more like the choice, precious stones Peter described—like the gemstones that were built into the temple Solomon constructed. God may show you how facets of who He's made you to be reflect the light of His glory. He may show you that He treasures you so deeply that He's engraved you on the palm of His hand (Isaiah 49:16).

If you're an overcomer, don't be surprised if God shows you a pure, white stone—like a pearl or an opal—with His own affectionate name for you written on it.

> *To him [her] who overcomes…I will give him [her] a white stone, and a new name written on the stone which no one knows but the one who receives it.*
> —Revelation 2:17

As God's living stone, you're not tossed to the side or forgotten. To the contrary, you're an integral part of the household of faith—called to serve as a priest. There, the Lord welcomes you to travel in communion with Jesus, our great Cornerstone. The Rock of Our Salvation.

As you move about the world from that sacred position, don't be surprised if the Holy Spirit begins to engrave His words of life on your heart. And stay ready for His cues to speak life into other people.

Can stones really speak?

Living stones can.

And that gem of a living stone could be you.

Lord, thank You for loving me so much. Help me to see myself as You see me. Polish me as the gemstone You made me to be. And guide me as I venture out in Jesus' name to help the world You love.

DISCUSSION QUESTIONS

1. Has God ever spoken to you through His Word, through another godly person, or personally? If so, write down and/or share the story. (The other side of all *Discussion Question* pages have been left blank to give you additional writing space as needed.)

ADDITIONAL NOTES

2. Earlier, did you think of anyone's story in Scripture that speaks to you? Share something specific about how you relate to that person from Bible Days.

ADDITIONAL NOTES

3. Has God used you as a living stone to help someone else? Has He brought a verse to mind or given you words of wisdom, encouragement, or comfort for anyone other than yourself?

   - If so, describe how you sense that God wants to speak through you (most often) and how you confirm what He's saying.

   - If not, have you asked God for that spiritual gifting? (Luke 11:13; 1 Corinthians 14:1, 3)

ADDITIONAL NOTES

ACTIVATIONS

Stone Sharing

Exercise your spiritual ears as you venture through the four steps of this first activity.

1. Ask God to put a single, encouraging word on your heart from the Bible.

2. Find two smooth stones. Paint that word you got on both—or order two stones, engraved with that word.

3. Share a stone. Ask God to bring someone to mind who would be helped by the message on that stone. Give the stone away with joy.

4. Keep the second stone to commemorate that inspired word God spoke to you. Remember to live by it yourself.

For more on this particular *Activation* as well as alternate ways to go about it, see Cheryl's unique take on stone sharing under *Bonus Activations*. This is one of those *Activations* that can bear repeating in a variety of fun and fruitful ways.

Each time you share a Spirit-led stone message, think of yourself as partnering with us and the growing body of living stones in our *These Stones* family. Stone-by-stone, it's a way to spread simple messages from God's Word with those who could be blessed to hear them.

You may only be led to put an inspired word or two on your stone. You may put a whole Scripture verse. But you can rest assured that not a single word from the mouth of God will ever return void.

Episode 1.1

listen

───────◆●◆───────

But Jesus answered, "I tell you, if these become silent, the stones will cry out!"

— Luke 19:40

There's nothing that feels quite as silent as the grave. If you've ever mourned a loved one, you get it. Experience tells you what someone like our main character McKenna would feel, staring at her mother's grave and the stones she left behind.

Though McKenna sits at that grave quietly, you can imagine what would be whirling through her mind, maybe because you've been there yourself. You might wonder how God could let your loved one get silenced so suddenly. You might know the grief of unresolved conflict. Maybe you blame or shame yourself for something you did or didn't do—or say before death parted you.

Even if you were in a functional, current relationship with that lost loved one, you've known the seeming finality of death. Everything in you may have ached to hear your loved one's voice again. Perhaps you longed to hear God's voice, assuring you that there was a way forward.

Maybe you saw or heard a spiritual signpost.

Like a message, crying out from a stone.

Though each person's story of loss is unique, grief is something we all come to experience. We can relate and find comfort by sharing our personal stories. We can help others by listening to their stories too.

I'll start with a bit of mine.

Last Words

As a child, I adored my grandparents. Still, I didn't ask much about their lives. Even after I'd grown up, they didn't volunteer their stories unprompted. But in time, I found that the simplest question could unlock golden nuggets of family history—fascinating stories they were delighted to share.

When Grandmom passed into the arms of her Savior at 98, I searched my mind. *What were her last words to me?* Ah, yes. We'd been on a cross-country call.

"I *love* you, Honey," Grandmom said. She accented and extended the word *love*—as if with her whole heart and soul leaned into that word. Then, almost as an afterthought, she buttoned the call with a wistful, "See you later."

Funny.

Grandmom had never ended visits or calls with that phrase. But she knew what it would mean to me. "See you later" was the parting phrase in my first film—spoken by a girl to her dying grandmother. It was a film that I'd dedicated to Grandmom and the God we loved, decades before.

Neither of us knew we'd never speak again, this side of eternity. Yet in retrospect, the memory of Grandmom's "See you later" comforted me.

So did the notes and prayers I found scrawled in the pages of her Bibles—some mentioning me by name. Those messages cried out to me, like Eliana's notes and videos cry out to McKenna in *These Stones*.

They were divine consolation.

Grandmom's inspired words broke through the silence of her grave. They assured me of the hope we have in Christ of being reunited one day. They underscored what a blessing it can be to listen to the people God graces us to know in this life.

Intentional listening may be among the most loving gifts you can give to another person. Think what a gift it is when God listens to you.

In my distress I called upon the LORD, and cried to my God for help; He heard my voice out of His temple, and my cry for help before Him came into His ears.

— Psalm 18:6

How About You?

Think about your experiences conversing with someone you may have parted ways with for some reason other than death. Maybe you parted on less-than-ideal terms. If more than one person comes to mind, just start with whoever you thought of first.

Picture that person's face.

Which of the following words best describes your relationship at the time you parted?

- loving
- healthy
- strained
- estranged

If you chose strained or estranged, ask:

- Have I really taken time to listen to that person?

- Have I asked meaningful questions about their life or what they're feeling?

- Have I stayed long enough to truly hear their point of view?

- Are there steps I could take to initiate healing?

Admittedly, that last question can be loaded when it's applied to certain people. Let's be wise and safe when it comes to highly toxic or dangerous relationships.

Even Jesus told His disciples that there was a time to shake the dust off their feet, when people refused to receive them or listen to what the Holy Spirit gave them to say (Matthew 10:14–16).

For now, let's focus on relationships that could be safely improved or healed through listening.

Or even a bit of humility.

Humble Pie à la Aaron

If there's any kingdom food group that's underrated, it's eating a slice of this relationship-repairing dessert. Maybe you haven't done anything wrong with that person. Like this episode's Courier Aaron, you might just be called to be the glue that helps piece another person's broken relationship back together.

Perhaps you're a mature believer like Aaron, who doesn't have a lot of recent slip-ups to confess. In our story, think how winsome Aaron is in citing his personal fails. Consider how that admission helps put Jonathan more at ease. Just that brief taste of Aaron's humanity opens Jonathan's ears to hear what Aaron has been given to say.

We've all made mistakes.

So let's own them.

Therefore, confess your sins to one another, and pray for one another so that you may be healed. The effective prayer of a righteous [person] can accomplish much.

—James 5:16

You may not think you've done anything wrong. You don't want to apologize insincerely. Still, you can refer to past mess-ups. You can say you're sorry it's taken so long for you to reconnect. You can say how much you regret how things went south in your last conversation.

Remember, our relationship enemy is also known as the *Accuser of the Brethren.* He opens by reading a judgy riot act of wrongs, then eggs us on to defensively follow suit. Friends, let's not do his prideful, destructive bidding. Instead, let's remember to take a healthy bite of humble pie in challenging conversations. Just that sincere taste of sweetness can help pave the way for relational healing.

Doing Damage Control

Of course, staying in healthy relationships is a two-way street. It means sharing our honest thoughts and being willing to listen intently as others share theirs.

The problem is, all too often, communication breaks down, as it did for Jonathan when his father kept talking over him—refusing to listen.

So Jonathan stopped listening too.

Jonathan went into long-term damage control. Despite his dying father's eventual attempts to make things right, he couldn't bring himself let go of their relational reins. Their rift made it that much harder to turn over control to a heavenly Father that Jonathan didn't trust to help.

Maybe you have a relationship like that.

You might sense a pattern where one person in the relationship dominates most conversations. Maybe you've got no hope of relating to that person in a balanced, healthy way. You've literally lost your voice in the relationship, like the stammer that Jonathan developed in our story.

Maybe you've even prayed for help. But you're stuck in self-preservation mode, nursing old wounds.

Actor, Jack Kelly had some insights to share with us from his preparation to play Jonathan.

"The stammer—I don't always know where it comes from. But I have the sense there's trauma there. There's the struggle to be heard, to get the word out. Literally."

—Jack Kelly (Jonathan)

So after years suffering the trauma of trying to get a word in—just to be heard—why does Jonathan resist his mother's pleas to visit his dying father who finally wants to hear from him? Why is it so hard to believe his mother when she says his father has changed?

"It's the layers of resistance. Because of pain. Nobody wants to be hurt. We avoid pain as human beings. And some of us become masters at it. The problem is it robs us of life. It robs us of so much. I wasn't willing to go. There's still a human ounce of resentment there that's holding on, which is so self-destructive. But it's what we humans do."

—Jack Kelly (Jonathan)

The sad truth? Jonathan let past pain steal the hope of present healing. He wasn't willing to try again. That long nursed but never-quite-healed wound became infected with resentment. A root of bitterness tangled around his soul (Hebrews 12:15).

Have you ever felt like Jonathan—where you can't get beyond a past offense?

Even after Aaron heard Jonathan's side, Jonathan still resisted visiting his father. It wasn't enough for Jonathan to see with his own eyes that Aaron was an emissary from God. Even after hearing how listening to God helped Aaron and Moses save their people from the tyranny of Pharaoh, Jonathan was still reluctant to try.

Here's an excerpt from that scene in our script.

JONATHAN
That's great for you and your
family, Aaron. But you don't know my
father.

AARON
Everyone has a Pharaoh to face.

How About You?

Like Jonathan, your challenging person may seem as formidable as a Pharaoh. Maybe years have passed since whatever caused the rift between you and that person. But the ache of that old, gaping wound makes you resist taking steps toward healing. Ask yourself:

- Do I want to be healed? Or am I clinging to past wounds as part of my present identity?

- Am I willing to do anything in my power to make peace? (Romans 12:18)

- Have I truly forgiven this person?

- Have I asked God to guide me and speak to me about this relationship? Am I listening to Him?

Consider three listening tips from the Bible.

This you know, my beloved brethren. But everyone must be quick to hear, slow to speak and slow to anger.
—James 1:19 [emphasis added]

Granted, many of us likely relate to Jonathan's desire to be heard. But let's take a moment to pull the logs out of our own eyes (Matthew 7:5). Let's examine our hearts for times we've been a bit more like Jonathan's father, Thomas.

- Are you the chattiest one in most conversations? Do you devote equal time to listening?

- Can you recall a time when you shut your ears to what the Holy Spirit was trying to say to you through a godly person in your life?

If you see listening lapses in yourself, let's get rid of any guilt right away. Let's tell God we're sorry and ask Him to help us be better listeners in the future.

Then, in the real-time of any new conflict that arises, exercise James 1:19's three great listening tips. It may seem challenging in the heat of that moment. But God can help you live out His inspired Word in a way that fosters healthier relationships.

Coordinated Communiques

Have you ever noticed that God often simulcasts similar messages to multiple hearers? As in our pilot episode, there are multiple characters who need to hear the same things for similar reasons.

McKenna needs to hear God's comforting words about losing her mother Eliana. But our heroine isn't the only one who's hurting. McKenna's dad has kept on numbing his grief with alcohol. He's been widowed.

Just as Rosie is about to be.

And they all need the same thing. They need someone to sit with them in their sorrow. Someone to care. Someone to listen. Someone to remind them God sees them—and that they're not alone.

Like Thomas, the dying need assurances too. The thing that troubled a dying friend of mine most was leaving her husband alone to raise their children.

My dying father endured horrific pain. But he ached most about what would happen to our ailing mother when he'd no longer be there to serve as her caregiver. He needed my assurances that we'd be a regular presence in her life and care.

You may be grieving yourself, like I was mourning my father. Still, I found it healing to spend time with my grieving mother. Admittedly, it can be challenging to sit with the bereaved. It's hard to know what to say. But that's our cue to do something that helps even more.

Lend a listening ear.

Remember: visiting widows and orphans is part of our calling. It has been defined as the very essence of sincere faith and adoration of our heavenly Father.

Pure and undefiled [worship] in the sight of our God and Father is this: to visit orphans and widows in their distress...
—James 1:27a

You see, the *listen* stone in our story wasn't just meant for Jonathan or his father. McKenna got her own stone as a divine directive for her life as well. One simple word cried out from that stone.

Listen.

That word helped McKenna to set her own pain aside, enough to sit with her grieving father. She didn't need to say much. She just needed to come alongside him, then open the door by asking: "How was your day?"

Spiritual Ears to Hear

As important as it is to love through listening intently to other people, above all, let's remember to actively practice listening to God. It's an expression of our pure love for Him. That's why He longs for us to cultivate a truly communicative relationship with Him, far beyond monologue prayers. Let's invite dialogue in the Spirit in light of these verses.

> *Your ears will hear a word behind you, saying, "This is the way, walk in it," whenever you turn to the right or to the left.*
> —Isaiah 30:21

> *My sheep hear My voice, and I know them, and they follow Me.*
>
> —John 10:27

Think about it. What if we truly accepted the gift of those verses? What a privilege it is for all those who follow Jesus to be on speaking and listening terms with God. Just like Jesus said we would be.

The Lord may speak to you through the Bible and the stories of people who lived in those days. That still, small voice of the Holy Spirit may come to your spiritual ears.

As in our story, He may even speak to you through godly human voices, living stones that defy the silence of the grave, crying out with messages of faith, hope, and love.

Father, thank You for always listening to me. Thank You for sending Jesus to open those lines of communication.

I confess I can be hard of hearing. Help me learn to listen more intently to the people You've placed in my life. Help me to be quick to listen and slow to speak or to anger. Give me courage to face my Pharaohs. Fill my spirit with the words I need to comfort those who are mourning.

And above all, help me to hear the sweet sound of Your voice. Speak, dear Lord. Your servant is listening.

DISCUSSION QUESTIONS

apply

1. What struggles or challenges did you relate to most in this episode?

2. Have you lost a loved one? If so, would you honor that person's memory by sharing a favorite anecdote from your relationship?

ADDITIONAL NOTES

3. What are your present listening skills like? Highlight any of these statements that apply to you.

   a) I have a hard time listening to others.
   b) I could use improvement.
   c) Average, I guess. I don't think about it.
   d) I'll only listen if people listen to me.
   e) People tell me I'm a good listener.
   f) I create opportunities to listen to others.
   g) I'd like to hear God's voice, but I haven't.
   h) I actively listen to and hear from the Holy Spirit when I read the Bible.
   i) I recognize and listen for God's voice, no matter what I'm doing in life.

Given your answers, in what ways can you work on becoming a better listener to other people and to God?

ADDITIONAL NOTES

4. Chew on a bit of humble pie with Aaron. Have you ever played second fiddle to someone else who got most of the credit, the way Aaron played second fiddle to Moses? How did that make you feel and what did the Lord teach you about humility through it?

5. What steps are you willing to take toward listening for and hearing God's voice? List steps that come to you below.

ADDITIONAL NOTES

ACTIVATIONS

Choose a Quiet Spot

Create a prayer closet like Eliana and her mother Louise used in *These Stones*. It doesn't have to be a literal closet. It just needs to be a quiet place where you can spend some one-on-one time with God every day—to read your Bible, talk to Him, and listen for His voice.

Befriend a Widow

In keeping James 1:27, strike up a listening friendship with an older widow, widower, or unmarried person. Look for those who are alone in life, someone who may not have as many friends or family. Persist, even if you have a bumpy start. Engage with that befriended widow or single person regularly. Reach out in person, by phone, by email, or snail mail. Ask questions and engage in meaningful conversations.

Practice Symbol Searching

The Bible is full of symbols to search. But for now, let's do a deeper dive into some symbols in *These Stones* to unearth their biblical meanings.

a) Watch the scene in *These Stones* when McKenna is in her mom's prayer closet and first hears a knock, then sees a door appear. Without reference materials, ask the Holy Spirit to tell you what that door and the knock represent. (Hint: if nothing comes to you or you want to confirm what you think you heard, check: John 10:7–9 and Revelation 3:20).

b) Level up your listening ears with this next challenge. Watch the scene where McKenna stumbles through the door and into the Corridor for the first time. Count the lights that come alongside her, lead her into Central Dispatch, then take their place in the starry expanse that appears before her. Ask God to speak to you about those lights and what they're meant to represent. (Hint: if you're unsure or would like to confirm what you think you're hearing with Scriptures, check these passages: Revelation 4:5, Isaiah 11:2, John 14:16–18, 26, 16:13.

c) Meditate on what you discovered in your symbol searches. Apply the truth of our allegory to how God has come alongside you in the Spirit.

FROM CHERYL

Episode 1.2

———◆●◆———

Train up a child in the way he should go. Even when he [grows] old he will not depart from it.

—Proverbs 22:6

W hen it comes to raising children, we often hear the phrase, "It takes a village." When we were kids growing up, we didn't understand how important building on a firm foundation was. The most vital part starts with being in personal relationship with the Rock of Our Salvation: Jesus Christ (Psalm 62:6).

Maturing as we age can be influenced by that village—those surrounding us. This could include family, friends, co-workers, mentors, teachers, pastors, and people in our communities. Even those who may consider us to be rivals or enemies.

61

As it says in Proverbs 27:17, *"Iron sharpens iron."*

Every one of those people can serve as the iron that sharpens us, contributing to our growth.

That iron reminds me of another portion of Scripture where it refers to the Word of God as being *"living and active, and sharper than any two-edged sword"* (Hebrews 4:12).

God's Word and the wisdom within those pages is one of the strongest tools that village around us can use to help us Grow—the word on the stone in our second episode.

My Need for Growth

I became a Christian at a very young age. So young, I don't remember how old I was.

When I was two years-old, my sister Heather, age five at the time, was paraded by a Sunday School teacher across the church stage—because she'd just committed her life to Christ in class. (This was news to our surprised parents, sitting in that congregation.)

I don't remember *my* moment like my sister had, since I grew up believing in Jesus as my Savior and going to church with my family.

During my teenage years, I had seasons of rebellion. As Eliana put it, they were going through McKenna's "achy, pushing away years." It caused growing pains between them.

During that era, I would have labeled myself a lukewarm Christian. Not overly committed, yet still a believer. I had a strong moral compass about some things, yet not others. I willingly told friends I was a Christian while teetering on that line between hot and cold.

When I was nineteen, I attended a recurring party we coined, "Pajama-Jammy-Jams." (We even planned ahead and packed our cozy flannels.)

My friends and I used to pile into living room sleepovers instead of driving home—especially if cherry wine coolers were involved.

I was fooled about my so-called witness to those friends. I'd get up the next morning, change out of my PJs, slip back into last night's clothes, and announce that I was leaving for church.

Picture it with me: tie-dyed leggings with every color imaginable, a neon pink tee—complete with a rhinestone clip to tie it off to one side. (I fit right into the eighties, even if it was the early nineties!)

At least I could slip up to the church balcony where the sardine-packed-downstairs-churchgoers wouldn't see me.

And then it happened.

The pastor gave one of *those* sermons.

"I know your deeds, that you are neither cold nor hot; I wish that you were cold or hot. 16 So because you are lukewarm, and neither hot nor cold, I will spit you out of My mouth."
—Revelation 3:15–16

I was as lukewarm as a teen could get, kidding myself about the strength of my personal relationship with God.

It was time to make a choice.

Did I want to grow in my relationship with God? Was I willing to make some changes?

The pastor ended the sermon with a call to action for those of us who needed to rededicate our lives to God.

"Make your way to the front of the stage."

Uh, oh. That's when I felt the nudge. You know the one. When your name flashes in supernatural lights at the altar.

"Really, Lord? In front of all these people? You know I'm wearing tie-dyed pink, blue, orange. This yellow and green...they glow!"

Yes. That's what God wanted. (Does the phrase "come as you are" ring any loud bells?)

Building upon the stone from our first episode— Listen—I knew that day I had to listen to God's voice, the call of His heart to "come back to Him."

My desire to obey—then change—through the growth God offered was stronger than any pride I was about to shatter, walking up front like a flashing, neon sign.

I didn't understand fully at the time. But in my heart, I wanted to grow beyond those spiritually immature years. Technically, I was an adult. Yet I'd followed my parents by becoming a believer as a child. But that day at the altar, it was my turn to choose to follow God and Jesus Christ as my Savior for myself.

I guess you could say that was *my* moment—like my sister's—parading across a stage.

It was also a huge turning point. Shortly after, God inspired me to write faith-based screenplays. He gave me a heart to change and impact the world through writing.

I wouldn't be here today, doing what I do writing faith-based television shows and movies, had I not answered God's call to grow.

It's similar to McKenna's experience as she moves from Episode 1.1 to 1.2. In the first episode, she was following her mother's calling. By this second episode, McKenna inches closer to starting her own relationship with God by showing up again at Central Dispatch.

How About You?

Have you ever found yourself in a place where you knew God wanted you to grow with Him, but the pull of the world was holding you back?

Have you been at a crossroads, where you sensed if you said "yes" to God, you could move to new heights with Him?

- Reflect on times when you've grown with God. What was going on to draw you closer to Him? (The seasons I grew most were during the darkest valleys of my life.)

- Next, think of times when you pulled away from God. What drew you away? (These are times when a growth spurt can halt in no time flat.)

- Are there times you didn't pull away on purpose, but you grew apart anyway? Like life got in the way and God became a lower priority. (Maybe you made less time for prayer, Bible reading, fellowship, or alone time with God.)

- Is there anything you can do to ensure you don't become stagnant or move backwards?

And I, [brothers and sisters], could not speak to you as spiritual [people], but as to [people] of flesh, as to infants in Christ. 2 I gave you milk to drink, not solid food; for you were not yet able to receive it. Indeed, even now you are not yet able.

—1 Corinthians 3:1–2

I'm thankful God wants us to grow, not stay on "milk" for the rest of our lives. He wants us to move to "solid food" that brings us into a deeper relationship and maturity.

To Grow or Not to Grow

In our show, Eliana had to watch McKenna make some choices she didn't agree with. Since McKenna was an adult, Eliana couldn't just demand obedience. She had to let her daughter grow up, even if it meant she'd fall sometimes.

Actress Charlene Amoia, who plays the role of Eliana, shared some insights into her character's dilemma about their dynamics.

> "I think Eliana's decisions always include praying a lot and checking in, trying to be there for her daughter, trying to let go so she doesn't push her away. Allow her to mature in her own time, at her own pace. So, I think it's this balancing act where we don't always do it right. Sometimes, we push too much. Or we let go too much."
>
> —Charlene Amoia (Eliana)

Before her death, Eliana had been creating videos for McKenna. She shot some of those after conflicts, to share a slice of advice for McKenna to hear in the future, especially if she became a mother one day.

Eliana recorded videos when she could see McKenna wasn't in a place to hear what she had to say *in that moment.* She wanted her daughter to have the option to learn from those videos later—when she could grow by hearing them.

You know what that reminds me of? God's Word.

It is always available to us. It can cut and divide right to the heart of a matter in no time. It's always at our fingertips to reach for, whenever we need advice, help, encouragement, direction—even correction.

But are we always ready to pick up that wealth of wisdom? Are there times when we may be tempted to rebel, so picking up the Bible is the last thing we want to do? Let's be real. Sometimes, we want to choose immaturity instead of growth. (I know I have!)

God gave us this treasure trove of wisdom to draw and grow from. But we're not always eager to hear from Him.

I used to joke that I had certain friends I'd go to when I wanted to be mature and challenged in all the best ways. Then I also had other friends to hang with or talk to when I wanted to be weak or lax on moral decisions—or when I didn't want to be corrected, let alone grow.

Anyone else relate?

We have such a gift in the Holy Spirit. He can act as a conscience, working through what God may be saying to us, through the Bible, advice from friends, or sermons.

But are we sometimes tempted to turn a deaf ear when it's not what we want to hear?

The alternative is to listen and obey. That's when a growth spurt can happen.

The Bible has wisdom for just about any situation where we might find ourselves. We just need to ask God for that discernment about what He wants to say about whatever "Pajama-Jammy-Jam" we're facing. Sometimes, it helps to have mature believers to talk to when we find ourselves stuck in those spiritual traffic jams. They can help us get back on track and nurture us to grow.

Like that pastor's altar call helped me.

I had a choice to ignore his call to the altar that Sunday. I'm thankful I didn't. It changed my life in all the best ways. It set me on the path to grow into God's calling on my life.

Encouraging Growth

After working in Holly's yard for a couple of days, winning her over with acts of service, Samuel and McKenna finally have a chance to talk to Holly about how she is hiding her son from the world.

Here are excerpts from their conversation:

```
                 SAMUEL
The world could use a lot more
Jimmys.


                  HOLLY
If only the world saw it that
way.


                 SAMUEL
I know it can be harsh out there.
But just think. Your son, being
who he is, can make the world a
better place. He can be a gift to
other people, given a chance.
```

Samuel shares that if his mother, Hannah, had not been willing to give him up to be used by God, he wouldn't have been able to do what God created him to do.

Actress, Denise Gossett, plays Jimmy's mother Holly, the recipient of Samuel and McKenna's help. Though Holly resisted at first, those acts of service opened her heart to hear what they had to say. Denise shares how she's worked to instill the value of small acts of kindness in her daughter:

> "Each little ripple of kindness spreads. That person that you held the door for may be having the worst day of their life and your little act of kindness can change them. Maybe they say hello to someone, then they smile at someone, and it just ripples. So that's what I think [*These Stones*] is going to do for everyone. It's a ripple."
>
> —Denise Gossett (Holly)

McKenna and Samuel's kindness in cleaning up Holly's yard, bringing her flowers, pruning shrubbery, listening to her concerns—those kindnesses had a ripple effect on Holly's and her son Jimmy's lives. This helped allow Jimmy to grow up, but also helped Holly to move forward in her own life.

Holly could have kept that door closed. She could have refused to have a conversation with McKenna and Samuel. Think of what she and her son would have missed out on, had she refused to open her door and heart to their help.

How About You?

- Have you been reluctant to crack open a Bible because you knew God would use it to tell you do something you didn't want to do?

- Have you ever felt like a plant in need of trimming? A mess of gangly branches—growing in wild directions like the bushes in Holly's yard?

- Has God shown up to "prune" you, so you could grow stronger and better? Or have you resisted His help because you didn't want to feel that pain of pruning?

John 15:1–17 is a great Bible passage that dives into how God is a loving gardener for us. Take a few minutes to review those verses and reflect on wherever you may be in that pruning process.

When God takes time to cut away unfruitful branches, it allows the rest of you to grow healthier and bear fruit. Try not to resist His pruning, even if it hurts at times.

Listen to Grow

In this episode, Samuel tells McKenna a story from his past while they're pruning Holly's yard (1 Samuel 3). He suggests that if McKenna wants a growth spurt, she should "lend an ear to what God has to say."

Remember when McKenna goes back to the thrift store and somehow, in her spirit, she sees those painted pots on the shelf? She senses she should give those to Holly to spruce up her front porch. Miriam even suggests she fill them with pansies. McKenna listens and is rewarded by Holly's joy as she shares that pansies are her favorite flowers.

That's what happens when we listen to God's leading. We can help others in ways that touch them far beyond what we could in our human insight or strength.

It's one of those acts that warms Holly's heart toward McKenna, Samuel, and Tanner after having sent the three of them packing the day before. McKenna's obedience to these promptings becomes an example of what can happen to any of us who enjoy an interactive, listening relationship with God.

It's the same way Samuel's interactive relationship with God changed and grew, right after he replied, *"Speak, for Your servant is listening"* (1 Samuel 3:10).

So much fruit comes from us when we do what God calls us to do. Like Eliana tells McKenna at the end of her video about the growing pains they're weathering: "It's all part of cultivating the beautiful fruit I know you'll come to bear."

Finally, Eliana ends the video with what should be encouraging advice for all of us.

"Take what God puts in your hands and run with it."

And whenever we do that—we're sure to grow.

Father, help me to grow in all areas of life. Personally, professionally, spiritually. If there are things I am doing to stunt my own growth, please help me overcome them.

Prune away the bad parts to make room for new growth. Open my eyes to those around me, those I can come alongside who need friends. Help me to be the kind of friend that can help others to grow too. To be the iron that sharpens iron.

DISCUSSION QUESTIONS

1. What struggles or challenges did you relate to most in this episode?

2. How does Eliana's desire to permit McKenna to "grow up" and be allowed to make mistakes mirror how God gives us freewill?

ADDITIONAL NOTES

3. Are there ways you may be guilty of excluding someone from your life or your usual group of friends? Is there something you can do to reach out to that person?

4. Who is in your "village"? Are they good influences or do they stunt your growth with the Lord?

5. Nosh on some humble pie with Courier Samuel. Samuel talks about not realizing God was trying to speak to him. Have you ever noticed after the fact that God was trying to get through to you about something—but it took you a while to realize it? How did you figure out that He was speaking?

ADDITIONAL NOTES

6. Can you recall a time that you knew God was speaking to you? Was it hard to act on what He said? If you did act on it, what was the result?

ADDITIONAL NOTES

ACTIVATIONS

venture

———•❖•———

Find Your *"Circle of Friends"*

Next time you're going out with friends, consider finding a café or coffee shop like *Circle of Friends* that hires adults with intellectual or developmental disabilities. They need the business and support. You'll get the chance to meet some wonderful people, working on making a living for themselves. You give them a chance to interact with others. You could make some new friends who will be very happy to serve you.

Brew it Forward

Our *Circle of Friends* coffee shop has an initiative called "Brew it Forward," where you can pre-pay for coffee for someone in a specific state of life. You write on a card the kind of person for whom this coffee will be free. (A single mom. A stressed-out college student.)

That act of kindness may really help someone having a bad day. If there's a local café that doesn't have an initiative like *Circle of Friends*, see if you can start one. Include a note of encouragement on the gift card.

The Invitation

Is there someone that you notice is often excluded? Invite that person to do something with you and your friends.

Cause a Ripple Effect with Kindness

Like actress Denise Gossett (Holly) suggests, do an act of kindness. It can be as simple as holding a door. Giving someone a smile.

Try more substantial acts of kindness too. Consider helping a widow or single mom with her out-of-control yard. There's nothing like pruning to illustrate the ways God helps us grow.

Dive into the Deep End

Pick an issue you are facing in your life where you feel like you need to grow. Write down why you feel that way and assess where you are right now.

Each day, ask God to show you one verse or passage that applies to that personal situation. Write a key verse down in a journal or on an index card.

Reread those verses at the end of the week to track progress and reassess. Do you feel any different than where you started? If you still have a long way to go, repeat the process the next week.

Episode 1.3

accept

———◆●◆———

"One of the most special episodes is in the middle of the series. Sometimes God tells us, 'No.' God closes the door that we really wanted to be opened. Whatever you're going through, the whole purpose of this is to get you to the other side."

—Madeline Carroll (McKenna)

This is one of those episodes I never wanted to write. The story I never wanted to accept as *my story*. I wanted a different answer. A different outcome.

First, allow me to take you back in time.

At fourteen, I dreamed of the day I could have a child of my own. I wanted a daughter who looked like me. Brown hair and eyes, olive complexion. I named her long before I got married, figuring whoever that man was would accept it.

Thankfully, I had the good sense not to do anything about those desires prematurely. This was one area I stuck to my convictions and genuinely wanted to follow God's plan for sex solely within the marital covenant. (For further study, see Hebrews 13:4, 1 Corinthians 6:13-18, 1 Corinthians 7:2, Acts 15:20, Colossians 3:5, 1 Thessalonians 4:3.)

Of course, I never imagined it would take until I was 39 years old to walk down the aisle. I was single much longer than I wanted—and quite annoyed—waiting on God to write my love story. By God's grace, I stayed in "wait mode" for activities that would allow me to conceive a baby.

Because Chris and I got married later in life, we had no time to waste trying to start a family. It never occurred to me that it wouldn't go well. Humorously, I *feared* it would happen right away before we had time to enjoy the "Just Us" season.

Once the decision was made to try to conceive—around eight months into our marriage—the "Nos" began.

Month after month.

At first, I wasn't overly concerned. If anything, it gave us more time alone. But as one cycle turned to the next (I kept meticulous count), I grew nervous. Then a myriad of health complications arrived. For me, all of them tied directly to my reproductive system. Chris also had five medical barriers to fathering a child.

Did that harm my faith that God had a plan for us to overcome those physical issues? Not at all. If anything, it charged my faith. I thought God would use this as an opportunity to show off.

Have you read verses in the Bible that talk about how children are a heritage from the Lord (Psalm 127:3), part of

His divine plan? How about His instruction to be fruitful and multiply (Genesis 1:28)?

Have you read how women conceiving were in God's domain—even those who experienced delays and closed wombs? Trust me: I did. Over and over. (Do Sarah, Rachel, Hannah, and Elizabeth sound familiar?)

So why wouldn't I believe God had that for us too? It's in His Word. Instead, my health issues grew worse and started to put my quality of life at risk.

Then, my doctor found it:

A benign tumor the size of a grapefruit.

Remember the scene where we're introduced to Drea in the medical waiting area? She's holding her ultrasound. We see she's distressed, but it isn't clear why yet. We assume, just like the adorable pregnant gal beside her, that her ultrasound pictures a baby.

But it doesn't.

That's what happened to me in real life.

I'll never forget that day, sitting in the medical waiting room, watching happy couples sashay out of their doctors' visits with strips of ultrasound images. They'd celebrate babies the sizes of raspberries, peaches, or lemons. All the while, I sat there, dying inside—holding my ultrasound photos that depicted the opposite.

A new life was *not* growing inside me.

What was growing could end me if I didn't get rid of it. Delaying surgery could cause complications. My doctor posed a solution. As Drea puts it, to take "the nuclear option." Get rid of everything that makes conceiving possible.

I don't have to tell you how horrible it was to face that decision. What if God wanted to fix this? Was I playing God by choosing my health and getting rid of it all? Was I closing a door on a miracle He still had in mind for us?

I wrestled with that decision for months, even as the tumor grew and I felt worse each day.

The LORD is near to the brokenhearted and saves those who are crushed in spirit.

—Psalm 34:18

How About You?

- Have you ever tried to have faith that God would answer a prayer, then realized you may be wrong?

- Did you realize God may have another plan in mind?

- Have you weathered a "No" from God, even when what you desired was good? How did you respond to Him?

If you have been hoping and praying for something and God seems to be saying "No," *you are not alone.*

It's okay to cry. To tell God how you feel about it. Share your disappointment. He knows those deep desires and that you'd come to have them, since before you were even born.

Nothing is a surprise to Him. At least take the time to be honest with Him about how you feel, even if it won't change your circumstances.

The Messy Middle

As I sensed God's ultimate answer for me, despite the faith I'd gripped for eight years while trying to conceive, I wrestled with anger.

Why? If the Bible is so clear that it's God's choice to give (or not give) children—to open or close wombs—why was I put into the "No" column?

Just like Drea complains to Sarah, why are there so many unwanted pregnancies? It was impossible for me to reconcile Scriptures with what God continued to allow around me.

Even witnessing God's blessings for others was hard to weather at times. Our young marrieds group started with one baby. By the time we moved out of state, there were thirty. Many were onto their second and third child by then. I didn't want any less for my friends' lives. But so many pregnancy announcements and baby shower invitations stung a bit.

I had been standing firmly on so many Scriptures for years. Not just ones I chose, but those other people had given to me. Including being told to just have Abraham and Sarah's faith that it would happen.

I clung to those words as if God were encouraging me through other people. In hindsight, I realize those words were simply other's innocent hopes for us.

I mistakenly clutched so tightly to the wrong verses that I'll highlight often misused ones below for you.

And He said to them, "Because of the littleness of your faith; for truly I say to you, if you have faith the size of a mustard seed, you will say to this mountain, 'Move from here to there,' and it will move; and nothing will be impossible for you."

—Matthew 17:20

Commit your way to the LORD, Trust also in Him, and He will do it.

—Psalm 37:5

Psalm 37:5 is often quoted as if God always gives us the desires of our hearts. Trust me. It didn't matter how many times—with my beyond "mustard seed-sized faith"—I told God my desire. It didn't matter how many times I spoke to the mountain; it unequivocally did not move.

I would add that verse I mentioned about children being a blessing from God to "No good thing does He withhold" (Psalm 84:11). You name it, I claimed it!

And yet, nothing changed our circumstances.

I kept our infertility a secret from a lot of people. Especially after we moved out of the young marrieds group to a new state. This was never something I talked about on social media. If anyone posted the question, "When are you going to have kids?" I'd delete it.

I was too embarrassed to discuss this most sensitive area of marital life. Telling our story through this series is our first public sharing of what we went through.

I'd like to candidly share about another part that made our journey worse. My only hope in sharing this part is that if you encounter someone going through something like this, you will be more sensitive to their situation.

I'll start by quoting an excerpt of dialogue from the Central Dispatch scene with Miriam, McKenna, and Sarah.

MCKENNA

```
Is there any chance that we're
supposed to talk to her about
adoption or foster care?
```

MIRIAM

This is not about pitching Drea
an alternate hope. People have to
mourn their losses, heal, before
they can move on.

Next time you encounter someone going through a trial like this, be "quick to hear, slow to speak" (James 1:19). Just be with them in their pain. Don't offer alternative solutions or pat phrases like "Just Adopt" when that is not the journey a couple is currently grappling with.

We heard that comment most often from couples with natural born children. It felt dismissive of what we were going through.

They'd say it like it's an easy solution. I'm sure it's well worth the cost (literally and emotionally) for couples who feel led that direction. But if you've walked with a friend through an adoption journey, you know.

Nothing about it is easy.

It's best for couples to decide *together* if they feel led in that direction and pray for God's help and provision every step of the way. Chris and I didn't feel that was the right choice for us.

To me, pitching that solution during someone's pain equates to telling a person who's just gone through a tough breakup that they will find a new mate one day. Or telling a woman who just suffered a miscarriage that she can always get pregnant again.

McKenna jumps to conclusions when she buys the "Baby's First Christmas" ornament. It's an example of her imposing her hopes on the situation. Her heart was in the right place, just like those who tried to give Chris and me their solutions. But the Christmas ornament was not a God-led gift for Drea in the way the potted pansies truly were for Holly.

Just like all of us, McKenna is human. Thankfully, she got spiritual direction from Miriam and didn't give a gift to Drea that could have caused more pain or given her false hope.

Some well-meaning friends gave gifts to me, in their innocent hopes for my future child. Unfortunately, those items became sources of anguish. Having to ultimately get rid of them was symbolic of the death of a long-held dream.

If you do relate to someone's pain, sharing that may be more helpful than offering solutions. I want to help others through shared mistakes or pains I've endured. It's that "messy middle" Miriam talks about.

SARAH
How is Drea going to feel when
she finds out that the Sarah who
got her miracle is here to
suggest that she give up?

MIRIAM
Has it ever occurred to you that
maybe you're not here because of
your happy ending? That perhaps
she needs you because of your
messy middle? If anyone can
understand the pain that Drea is
in watching everyone around her
get pregnant except her...it's
you.

Actress Micah Lynn Hanson (*Disciples in the Moonlight*), had some insights to share about playing Sarah.

"I'm very much like [Sarah] in real life in the sense that I will get the blessing that I've asked for and then I will still royally screw up. You think you've learned so much and you trust God, and then it's like you trust Him for a certain amount of time. Then, 'Okay, well, that didn't happen. So, I'm going to do it my own way.' There have been things that I'm like, 'Okay, God, I know You promised this for me, and it hasn't happened. I don't see the promise fulfilled yet.' I've tried to do it my own way a couple times and it doesn't [work]."

— Micah Lynn Hanson (Sarah)

I was blessed when Erin Bethea (who played Kirk Cameron's wife in the movie, *Fireproof*) accepted my offer to play the role of me (as Drea). When she was asked what her favorite line of dialogue was, she pinpointed one that pierces.

He could fix this if He wanted to.

Erin shares:

"The reason I love that line is because I think so many people feel that way about God in their circumstances. They feel like they can't reconcile that a loving God would allow suffering or allow unhappiness to exist in the world.

I think sometimes we're afraid to say that we're mad at God, or disappointed, or that we feel that He's let us down in some way. So, when [Drea] speaks those words out loud, it's important.

He is a loving Father. And we are allowed to tell Him we disagree, that we wish it were otherwise. Faith is not that we believe in God because He works everything out for us."

— Erin Bethea (Drea)

How About You?

- Have you ever tried to quote a Scripture repeatedly, hoping it would change your life? (That's okay if God leads you to. If not, it can derail you and your faith.)

- Has anyone used a Scripture in your life that ended up not applying in the way you'd wanted? How did you cope with that? (It can be painful to hang hope on someone else's desires for us, especially if it's not God's plan.)

- Are you currently holding onto something that God may not have for you? (Take some time to reflect on this. See if there are any desires in your life right now that you are holding too tightly.)

Sometimes, it may not be that God doesn't have it for us. But we can make our dreams too important, even more than God Himself. He may be waiting on us to surrender that desire, to not allow it to be an idol any longer.

- Have you been guilty of giving someone a word of encouragement that might have been detrimental to them? Was it based on your hopes and not God's will for their lives? Did it make it harder for them to accept a "No" from God?

I hope this helps us all to remember to pray before speaking about sensitive issues. To seek God first about His will and not offer someone false hopes.

The Stage of Acceptance

I stopped counting our monthly "Nos" sometime after Cycle #102. In 2020, I caved in to the idea of scheduling surgery, to get rid of all hope and the parts of my body necessary to conceive. I figured if God had a last-minute plan, He could fix it. (After all, I was required to take a pregnancy test right before surgery.)

But God didn't change anything. Not even when He got more time, because surgery was postponed due to the pandemic. Unfortunately, those extra four months allowed my condition to worsen. The tumor grew bigger. So much that there were several complications in surgery that likely would not have happened four months earlier.

But finally, it was over.

Including my dreams.

I believed once it was finished, I'd be able to accept my situation and move on quickly.

I was wrong.

Accept is the final stage of grief. I had more steps to travel before I'd feel emotionally healed. Surgery was not the formula I'd expected, to get on with life, back on track with God, and feel better.

I still held a lot of anger against God for "letting me down" (in my opinion).

One year later, to the exact date of surgery, I was at the Christian Worldview Film Festival organized by the Kendrick Brothers (*Facing the Giants, War Room, Fireproof*). There is not enough space in this book to explain the significance of that time, the divinely orchestrated conversations God allowed me to have there. The healing moments, the prayers, the listening ears of some incredible women of God.

That was also the week God whispered in my spirit that I was to start a new company with my friend, Jeanette Towne (an Executive Producer of our show). Instead of making my passion project, *Never the Bride*, like we expected, God nudged me to redirect our efforts to create *These Stones* as a TV series, in that season of time. It was based on a book manuscript written by Jeanette's pastor Tim Stevenson and the woman who became his co-writer, Peggy Porter.

Through that process, God led me to write our story.

Yes. This private one.

I had been so embarrassed for so long. So hidden. But the time had come to share what happened. If I hadn't listened to God's leading, I'm not sure where I would be on my journey to *Accept*.

I can't tell you how many times I've been told by script readers and viewers of *These Stones* that this episode meant the most to them, because they've weathered a "No" from God. We commonly hear this episode is the most relatable to life.

The truth is, we don't always get what we want. Our prayers are not always answered the way we hope. Despite that, we need to be okay with God.

God can take our anger, our truth about how we feel. But we've also got to climb out of those negative feelings like anger and accept that He truly knows what is best for us.

Even when His answer is "No."

I realized, in needing surgery, I got my "No." What I wanted to illustrate with this episode is that sometimes, when God tangibly gives us a "No," it is actually a gift.

That "No" I got was what allowed me to move toward acceptance and move on with my life. It's what allows Drea to move on with her husband. In her case, she was at risk of losing Brock. (That was one story departure from real life; thankfully, my marriage was never in jeopardy.)

Sarah says to Drea, "You can accept this answer as the gift it's meant to be. You can close this door in faith."

I had to get to that place too. Acceptance wasn't instant. But that "No" from God was a start. I'm thankful to say I am fully healed now. I have finally stopped asking why. I no longer feel the pain of it.

Being able to write about pain has always been a great coping device. One of my favorite verses is Romans 8:28. This was my chance to live it out.

> *And we know that God causes all things to work together for good to those who love God, to those who are called according to His purpose.*
> —Romans 8:28

God loved me all along the way, as I struggled to make peace with His choices. He sent me friends, family, and mentors to help.

Plus, God gave me that incredible gift of my husband, Chris.

I was never alone.

I hope if you've struggled with anything like I did, you will find your way back to peace and acceptance with God.

No matter what.

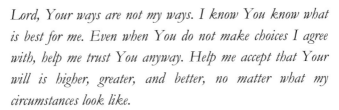

Lord, Your ways are not my ways. I know You know what is best for me. Even when You do not make choices I agree with, help me trust You anyway. Help me accept that Your will is higher, greater, and better, no matter what my circumstances look like.

If I can minister to someone because of my "messy middle," help my pain become my testimony. Anything I've been through is redeemed when You allow me to help someone else. Let Proverbs 3:5 be the song of my heart, which reminds me to trust in You and not to lean on my understanding.

DISCUSSION QUESTIONS

1. What struggles or challenges did you relate to most in this episode?

2. Has God ever said "No" to something you asked for, that later you found yourself very thankful you didn't get?

3. Share some humble pie with Sarah. Sarah admits to Drea she treated Hagar horribly in the past. Have you ever treated someone badly because they got a blessing that you wanted? Do you fight jealousy when God blesses other people?

ADDITIONAL NOTES

4. If you thought of a time when you misapplied a Bible verse or story to your life or someone else's, what would have been a more appropriate verse or story for that situation? Which Bible "Courier" would have been best for that? Why?

5. Read multiple translations of Matthew 11:6. Why do you think Jesus wanted to caution us to not fall away because of Him? Have you ever been tempted to walk away because of God's choices for you?

ADDITIONAL NOTES

ACTIVATIONS

venture

———◆●◆———

"Milestones with God" Chart

Read Psalm 77. It is a great example of a person (Asaph) in distress who then recounts God's past faithfulness to carry him through a difficult time. You can hear the Psalmist's tone going from depressed to hopeful as he stopped to remember all the times God had been there for him in the past. Those "milestone" moments he dwelled on helped to carry him through new challenges.

Now it's your turn. Create a *Milestones with God* chart of your life history. Record key dates and events. Ones that detail past times when God has tangibly shown up for you. Moments you've seen His faithfulness, answered prayers, protection, rescues, or miracles. Remembering times God has been there for you will remind you He hasn't left you in your current challenges. Use this record to build your faith.

I shall remember the deeds of the LORD; I will certainly remember Your wonders of old.

—Psalm 77:11

Act of Faith

Just because this episode highlights a time God's answer was "No" doesn't mean there aren't times He plans to answer a prayer as requested with a resounding "Yes."

Even so, God may require you to do something that makes room for Him to move you forward. Is there an act of faith God is calling you to do? Ask Him for your next steps.

EPISODE 1.4

grace

---◆●◆---

For by grace you have been saved through faith; and that not of yourselves, it is the gift of God; 9 not a result of works, so that no one may boast.

—Ephesians 2:8–9

When we first started developing six stories for the freshman season of *These Stones*, our fourth episode was the first one I wanted to write. It's always been on my heart to write a story about the detriments of not waiting on marriage for sex. This show gave me the opportunity to do that.

So often, especially when talking to teenagers, I see the adults in their lives focused on avoiding two consequences: unwanted pregnancy and sexually transmitted diseases.

Public schools will teach "safe sex" long before they'll share the high value of abstinence. They equate waiting with antiquated "religious" values.

But what about the emotional consequences? Why only equip young people with "protection" for their bodies but not their hearts?

As I like to say:

There is no condom for your heart.

These choices can erode self-esteem, especially in young women who might choose sex to keep a boyfriend they fear they'll lose if they don't give into him.

Just like our Katie.

Young people may not understand that their choices matter—not only in the present—but also to their future.

The Bible makes it clear this kind of sin harms us in more ways than other sins.

Flee [sexual] immorality. Every other sin that man commits is outside the body, but the immoral man sins against his own body.

—1 Corinthians 6:18

I'm so thankful that God is a God of abundant grace. Like the opening verse of this episode's chapter says, we have been saved by grace and not any works we can do.

This includes the choice to abstain from sin.

No matter what mistakes we've made in the past, God is there to offer His forgiving grace when we ask Him with a repentant heart.

My Way-Too Personal Story

Trust me when I say I'm not judgmental toward those who've made mistakes in this area of life by stepping outside of God's plan.

I've needed plenty of grace from God for my own failures in other areas. That's why I completely understand if this is a part of your life that could benefit from God's covering of grace. However, I am very thankful I remained abstinent before marriage.

One thing that helped me wait is I had enough examples around me who did *not* wait. They became cautionary tales to me as I observed—or even helped them through—some of their painful consequences.

Their consequences made me pause before following their paths, even at the urging of many to "go ahead and give in." You know the annoying, "Everyone else is doing it" promptings. (I was a teen in an era when it wasn't as common or as pressurized as it is now. It's hard for me to imagine how difficult it is for young adults growing up today.)

At times, I took the opposite approach. I was even "anti-peer-pressure" in a way that worked in my favor. (Sometimes, even if I wanted to do something, I wouldn't, simply because someone tried to push me.)

This was especially the case after I had a front row seat to the painful consequences some people in my life suffered. Like when the boyfriend she thought would be in her life forever walked away after he got his physical fill. Even back then, people didn't need social media to bully, spread rumors, or damage reputations. I wanted none of that.

I was extremely ambitious and future-minded about my career aspirations in theater and films. I didn't want bad relationships (or the consequences of them) getting in my way.

On the other hand, I also battled anxieties related to men that helped me stick to my personal vow to wait for marriage. My fears worked in my favor (as I share in my autobiography, *Finally Fearless*)—admittedly even more than my desire to please God. Some guys even told me I gave off a "stay away from me" vibe.

That explains why I relate more to McKenna in this episode than Katie. But I also understand how difficult it is, especially these days, to hold that line.

How About You?

- What choices have you made in relationships about how to handle the physical side of things?

- If you're married now, but made mistakes in the past, do you still struggle with not condemning yourself for those past mistakes? Is there anything you feel led to pray, confess, or share with God or others to help you seek forgiveness? (This will help reinforce in your heart that the slate is wiped clean.)

- If you are currently single, have you made choices you are not proud of? (If you haven't already, now would be a great time to seek God's forgiveness and make the decision in advance of any future temptations to not go there again.)

- Are you open to praying to ask God for strength to make new choices? (If you are currently living in a relationship outside of God's plan, I know He is waiting for you with open arms to help lead you through the next steps. He's always ready with a forgiving heart and will help us move forward with Him.)

Keep in mind, it's never too late to turn away from sin and take the way out that God offers to you.

No temptation has overtaken you except something common to [human beings]; and God is faithful, who will not allow you to be tempted beyond what you are able, but with the temptation will provide the way of escape also, so that you will be able to endure it.

—1 Corinthians 10:13

Graffiti Covered Walls

Singer/songwriter Katherine Shepler plays Katie in this episode. When I first heard Katherine's song *Graffiti*, I was immediately struck by the lyrics. I had no idea what the story behind the song was. But I loved the symbolism.

I asked Katherine if I could fictionalize what the song was about and have this character act out writing her song. I was thankful Katherine not only said yes to using her beautiful song this way—but that she was also willing to play this emotionally challenging role for us.

Already embedded in the song was the story of a young woman willing to cry out to God to help her stop covering up her sin. Covering up was only making life more painful.

For all of us, unconfessed sin only keeps us in bondage and out of deep fellowship with God.

To follow are a few excerpts from Katherine's lyrics.

I was running from a failure
Towards the fire of regret
I was covered in the colors
Of a pain I'd never felt.

They say you can't put a bandage on a bullet
And you can't live like you didn't do it.
And all these Graffiti covered walls
Pictures of who I have become

Paintings on pain I thought was gone
Have to come down
Before I can see You
I want to see You.

So when I realize I am lost
I look at Your arms stretched out on the cross.

And all these graffiti covered walls
Won't keep me hiding anymore

Each day I'll see what I have drawn
And heal from the pain until it's gone.

Incredible imagery, isn't it?

Rahab felt like the perfect Bible Courier to step into Katie's life. Having lived as a prostitute for a time, "Ms. Rae" is able to relate to Katie with great understanding.

Katherine shares about this:

"There were people thousands of years ago who were experiencing the same things, who have lessons they can teach and pour into you. I love the theme of mentorship—where the Bible characters give advice to the present-day people. Just the wisdom you can glean from people who have walked through a similar experience. And the humility it requires to admit, 'Hey, I need someone to help me.'"

—Katherine Shepler (Katie)

One of the most important things to understand is that *change is possible*. Forgiveness and grace are available. We don't have to believe the lie that once you've made a mistake, there's no point in trying to turn from that sin because you've already messed up or that you're damaged beyond repair.

Katie struggles to believe this at first. Here's an excerpt from her conversation with Rahab.

                    KATIE
I can't seem to stop. And what's
the use anyway? I'm already
wrecked.

RAHAB

What if you could start over
again, wipe the slate clean?

KATIE

I can't get back what I've
already lost. I don't see how
that's possible.

Rahab shares the story of her promiscuous past, then how she was rescued, and turned from her old ways. Joshua 2 & 6 recount the beautiful story about the grace that was offered to Rahab and her family. It's a grace Rahab says is available to Katie too.

When we go to God and confess, He encourages us to bring everything we tried to keep hidden out into the open. It's just like what 1 Peter 2:9b says: *"[God] called you out of darkness into His marvelous light."*

That's where healing can begin. And the most beautiful "art" can come from those strokes of God's redeeming paint brush, covering our sin.

Katie no longer has to keep adding layers of dark paint to herself to cover what feels ugly beneath. Instead, she steps out into the open. She's able to be honest with Rahab and McKenna first, then later with her mother. That allows her transformation to continue throughout her song, which becomes a life-changing confession.

One of my favorite moments in this whole series is when Katie walks out onto the stage into that light and sings for an audience of One:

Jesus.

No Debt Due

During a flashback scene, McKenna's mom, Eliana, gives McKenna a very important piece of advice as she's preparing to leave on a date.

> ELIANA
>
> Remember, Honey. Whatever tab he picks up, you owe him nothing.

Eliana's line was inspired by a discussion I had with my students in a university writing class. I asked them what effects Hollywood movies or television series have had on their lives. A few young women spoke up in ways that broke my heart.

They said it felt like TV and movies have contributed to creating a "hook up" culture. Shows and films have trained guys to think that buying them dinner entitles them to sex afterward.

My heart sank for them. Dinner pays for sex? That's not even as much as a prostitute would make. No way. And I hope anyone reading this book or watching our show will help young people understand that this is a devious lie of the enemy.

It saddens me that Hollywood has contributed to the normalizing of sexual sin. It makes it that much harder for people who want to wait for marriage. They're made to feel like outcasts or as if something is wrong with them if they aren't having sex like so many others.

I hate that the pressure—even the expectation—is there, and that it's become rare for someone to wait. Even among those who believe.

Thankfully, God's grace is available to us all, no matter what we've done.

And He has said to me, "My grace is sufficient for you, for power is perfected in weakness."

—2 Corinthians 12:9a

How About You?

- Have your sexual choices been influenced by TV shows or movies? Next time you watch mainstream TV, pay attention to the messaging related to sex. Are they normalizing what God calls sinful? Are they mocking those who wait? Is waiting even a thing? Or is it assumed "everyone is doing it"—so abstinence isn't even part of the conversation?

- In our story, Rahab and McKenna showed up for Katie. Is there a mentor you can go to if you are struggling in this area? Is there someone you can trust not to judge you, but to help you move in a spiritually healthier direction?

This episode is focused on teenagers, but God's Word applies to adults as well. I'm truly thankful I ignored friends who told me, as I got older, I had waited "long enough."

- Even if you don't struggle with sexual sin, is there another sin you're trying to cover or pretend isn't there?

- What steps can you take to bring that sin to light so you can deal with it, heal, and move forward?

A Symbolic Reminder

A key moment of grace in this episode comes from McKenna, as she gently comes alongside Katie.

MCKENNA

```
You're not alone. There are
things I keep punishing myself
for too, like that wound you keep
reopening. But I'm thinking maybe
we can help each other stay
strong if either of us starts to
get weak.
    (hands Katie a red bracelet)
This bracelet is for you, Katie.
When you see it, maybe it'll
remind you to wait. Or if you
fail, at least not to hurt
yourself again. Instead, you can
call me.
```

Rahab also wears a scarlet cord to represent when she was rescued from her sinful past by God's people. That's why McKenna gives Katie that "scarlet-corded" bracelet, as a reminder not to fall into sexual sin again. But if Katie does, McKenna suggests that Katie could call her, rather than resorting to self-harm.

Finally, McKenna offers something those of us who are older or stronger in this area should consider. She offers to be an accountability partner. *These Stones* is all about helping other people. Sometimes that means coming alongside other people to lovingly reinforce their growth over time.

I have to say that my co-author of this book, Susan, was one of my strongest accountability partners. She's someone I consider to be a gift from God.

Susan entered my life when I was a teenager, admiring her work on television. Her professional mentorship turned to a personal friendship as I grew up and moved to Los Angeles to chase my dream of screenwriting. She mentored me through quite a few tough relationships, breakups, and friendships with guys when I wondered where they would go.

In every single case, she encouraged me to stay the course. To seek God's direction. To follow God's plan physically and even emotionally—when I'd get tempted to grow too attached to someone before I understood God's plan for our future.

Just like Katie and I needed, all of us need wiser counselors. If not for friends and mentors like Susan, there is no telling what kinds of harmful choices I might have made.

That's why we modeled godly mentorship in our story, with Miriam taking McKenna under her wing. Let Miriam's maternal wisdom and compassion be an example to you as you follow Jesus by discipling others.

If you recall, McKenna royally messed up, jeopardizing Rahab's ability to help Katie. But Miriam was able to see past the offense. She discerned that McKenna's repentant heart was in the right place. Miriam acknowledged that she'd made mistakes herself.

Then, remember what Miriam said? She told McKenna, "I'm starting to see a little more of your mom in you." Miriam didn't point to herself. Instead, Miriam humbly spoke of the woman whose big shoes McKenna was trying to fill: her godly mother, Eliana.

For McKenna, nothing could have meant more.

As you come alongside others, I encourage you to take after Miriam in that way. Have the humility to admit you've made mistakes too. And ask the Lord to give you the words to help encourage your mentees by noting any progress you see. Remind your mentees that God is still there. And He hasn't given up on them.

In the song, *Graffiti*, there's a lyric that says:

You say You're not done with me yet.

I am so thankful God isn't finished with any of us. He doesn't give up on us. He's always ready to extend a hand of grace—to give you a future and a hope (Jeremiah 29:11).

Opportunities will come to make new choices, no matter what you've done in the past.

> *For of His fullness we have all received, and grace upon grace.*
> 17 *For the Law was given through Moses; grace and truth were realized through Jesus Christ.*
>
> —John 1:16–17

———◆●◆———

Father, I know I'm not perfect. I've made mistakes in the past and I will again. I ask You to give me the strength to turn from sin. Give me a strong conscience to know when I'm being tempted or anything I'm doing that may open doors to temptation.

Help me make good choices, going forward. Thank You for the abundant grace You offer me daily. What You've put in Your Word is for my good, not just to deprive me of what seems fun at first. As my loving Father, You always know what is best.

DISCUSSION QUESTIONS

apply

———•———

1. What struggles or challenges did you relate to most in this episode?

2. As Katie faces self-loathing, she adopts the destructive habit of cutting. Are there habits you've developed that could be considered damaging to your health—in body, mind, or spirit? If so, can you pinpoint the underlying cause, like in Katie's case, her choice to be sexually active before marriage? If you're not sure, ask God to reveal it to you.

ADDITIONAL NOTES

3. Steal away for some humble pie with our Courier Rahab. Rahab admits that she had *past* shame over things she let men do when she was a prostitute. We see in the way she relates to Katie that she feels completely forgiven and covered by grace. Have you asked forgiveness for things that you have a hard time letting go of? What can you learn from Rahab's response to being covered by grace?

4. Is there anything you feel shame about that you have not asked forgiveness for yet? If so, consider taking time to do that privately or in your group if you feel comfortable. It's the key that will unlock God's abundant grace.

5. Is there anyone in your life who needs an extension of grace, even in the midst of their mistakes or sins? If so, is there something God may want to inspire you to do, to help bring them back to healthy choices in their lives?

ADDITIONAL NOTES

ACTIVATIONS

Seek Mentors

Katherine Shepler (Katie) talks about the importance of having mentors to walk you through issues. Who are your mentors? Is there an area of life you need mentorship in? If so, could you start to seek out someone who's been through something you are facing, who may be willing to offer godly, biblical wisdom and counsel?

Seek to Mentor

What areas of life could you step up in and mentor someone else? Think through your life experiences, especially where you've overcome a specific challenge or something you've healed from. Do you have helpful tools to offer someone struggling, based on your experience?

Artistic Expression

Graffiti is a beautiful song of confession, sharing remorse, and giving gratitude to God, for His grace and forgiveness. Write song lyrics or a poem, expressing something you've been through. You could write this like a Psalm, many of which are prayers to God. If you have interest in filmmaking, you could turn your story into a film script. Or a novel. You could paint a canvas with images that express your heart.

Find a Symbolic Memento

Like McKenna gives Katie the red bracelet to remind her not to cut herself again, is there something you could buy or make that can be with you as a reminder? It can be a piece of jewelry that means something to you about what you don't want to forget.

Soak in a Redeeming Song

Take the time now to find Katherine's song, *Graffiti* online. Listen to the whole thing. Soak in it. Put it on repeat. Think through her lyrics and consider if there's anything you relate to in there.

Episode 1.5

But speaking the truth in love, we are to grow up in all aspects into Him who is the head, even, Christ...
—Ephesians 4:15

In my youth, I became a bit of a prodigal for my parents—like a mid-teens version of our 22-year-old McKenna. Since childhood, Mom and Dad had raised me on the truth of the Bible, just as McKenna's mom raised her in our story.

Technically, I believed. But like McKenna, that head knowledge hadn't migrated to my heart. I hadn't chosen to follow Jesus for myself yet. And I wasn't ready to give control of my life to God—not when I was already eager to push past the boundaries my parents drew for me.

In my opinion, my parents were overly protective. Why couldn't they give me more freedom, like my friends had?

I mean, I was 16—not a child anymore.

Or so I thought.

To be fair, my parents had gradually given me a bit more rope—just not as much as I wanted. But the tastes of freedom I did get were intoxicating. The rush of pushing boundaries to get what I wanted was as addictive as any drug.

Problem was, I'd get caught. My parents didn't track me. They'd just pray. And the truth of whatever I'd done would get back to them through friends. My sin would rat me out.

This did nothing for my arm's length association with God. It also undermined my parents' ability to trust me. And our once-loving family relationship suffered as a result.

Groundings had me impatiently counting the days until I could regain at least some liberty. I never became addicted to opioids like Olivia or to alcohol like McKenna's dad, Andrew. But taking control of my personal freedoms? That became my rogue habit of choice.

Kind of like it was for McKenna.

Maybe you've been there too.

Truth or Dare

Sprung from my latest grounding, I asked my mom if I could ride with my friend Julie to a Bible study. The rub? My parents didn't allow me to ride with newly licensed drivers.

And Julie's license was hot off the presses.

So. How could I spin the truth to my advantage?

I laid it on thick about my legit interest to learn about the Bible and hang with a couple of on-fire believers we'd see at the study. It would only be a few miles in Julie's mom's tank-like Cadillac. Straight there, straight back, I promised.

Finally, Mom said I could go.

Before very long, Julie pulled into our driveway. To my surprise and my mother's alarm, Julie arrived in a rented, sparkly blue convertible. Turns out the Caddy was in the shop.

Quickly, I reiterated my promise. Straight to the Bible study, straight back. I gave Mom my word, fully intending to keep it.

But here's the thing. We arrived at the Bible study house 20 minutes early. Our friend Cindy hopped into the back seat and lit up for a nicotine fix with Julie. The two of them cooked up the idea of us taking the ragtop out for a spin to the beach during the 20 minutes we had free.

Dare I?

Sure, I could have opted out. But the allure of that restraint-free joyride with my gal-pals got the better of me. We'd be back in plenty of time. My parents would never find out, right? So off we drove—hair whipping in the wind of that open convertible.

Free as teenaged birds.

As we neared the beach, we pulled to a stop by a bunch of young guys in a truck. Something about the high of that moment had us flirting with those guys shamelessly. I swung around to share a laugh with Cindy, then froze in shock.

There was my dad—in the sedan right behind us.

Busted.

Once again, my father hadn't tracked me. He was just innocently driving my brother to a scout troop meeting.

Frantically, I ducked onto the passenger floorboard. Cindy jumped over my seat and sat there to cover me. The light turned green, so Julie whipped right. Wonkily, she ran over the curb in the process (illustrating why my parents didn't let me ride with new drivers).

Of course, any attempt to hide was futile in that open convertible. I'd seen my father's face and he'd seen mine. There was nothing left to do but go home and face Mom.

More on that aftermath later.

Opportunity Knocks

Like me, McKenna dearly loved her mom. And she'd tasted even more freedoms while away at college. She'd already made her own choices about seeing that new beau Dylan and the dream-building doors he promised to open for her—choices her dad fully supported.

Jokingly, McKenna chalked up her mother's concerns to worry. Too quickly, McKenna forgot about the door that her spiritually sensitive mom said would open to her—a door that would lead McKenna into all that she was meant to be.

In the aftermath of Eliana's death, both McKenna and her dad privately blamed themselves. The father-daughter camaraderie they'd once enjoyed devolved into walking the eggshells of shame. How could they lance that wound, let alone talk honestly with each other?

There seemed no way for McKenna to tell her spiritually jaded father the truth about her growing faith. Not with him drinking every night.

How About You?

Perhaps you or a loved one struggle with alcohol or drug abuse like Andrew or Olivia in *These Stones*.

Take a moment to examine yourself before God, in the privacy of your heart.

Ask yourself this question:

- Has honest communication broken down with God or a human relationship because of some sort of addictive or harmful behavior pattern?

Controlling Behaviors

You and I may not have substance abuse problems, like McKenna's dad or Olivia. Still, the natural chemical highs of dopamine can hook any of us to a host of habits that give us pleasure. You know that hit of euphoria when you finally get something you've really wanted?

That's the dopamine happy dance.

Now, God created dopamine as a very good thing. It operates like a natural messenger to our brains. He made dopamine to support many healthy bodily functions—like memory and movement, sleeping and waking.

Dopamine was also designed to serve as an internal motivation/reward system. It motivates us to do things we need to do to survive—like eat, drink, and exercise. It also contributes to that rewarding feeling we get from helping others—the way McKenna does with the Program.

When we sense danger, dopamine tag-teams with its cousin adrenaline to alert the tiny emotional command center of our brains. In a flash, it heats up. This triggers the fight or flight energy we need to protect ourselves—from physical or emotional peril.

The exact same rush of brain chemistry fires up when we sense a door of opportunity opening to us—like McKenna's audition for that guy's manager. That's why nerves can get the better of us over anything we really want to go well.

So why all this talk about brain chemistry?

As believers, it's wise to examine what's controlling us— even beyond "controlled substances" like Olivia's opioids or Andrew's alcohol. Day-by-day we need to ask ourselves:

Am I living in the self-control of the Spirit or riding on overactive brain chemistry?

We should face how easily we can become dependent on behaviors that trigger excess dopamine and adrenaline hits. That way, we'll be more likely to recognize when we're co-opting brain chemistry into fueling destructive addictions.

Beyond substance abuse, there are so many other, less obvious ways we can become addicted to dopamine pleasure hits. Excessive video-gaming, risk or thrill-seeking, gambling, food addictions, pornography, overspending, and many other harmful patterns can take over.

If you've ever gotten anxious about not enough "likes" on social media, you know how addictive getting approval from friends and followers can be. Even the desire to control ourselves or others through lies and manipulations can have us driving under that brain chemistry-induced influence.

These behaviors may seem acceptable to some. They may not be illegal. But they're not good for us.

Remember:

All things are [legal] for me, but not all things are profitable. All things are [legal] for me, but I will not be mastered by anything.

—1 Corinthians 6:12

All those potentially addictive behaviors have one thing in common. They're a fast track to derailing your relationship with God and other people. They compromise our ability to love ourselves and live truthfully. They make us less likely to remain faithful to our word.

Like I was with that joyride.

Best Laid Plans

Have you ever made New Year's Resolutions? You hype yourself up and write it all down. You celebrate the clean slate that January 1st gives you. You wake up determined to master whatever harmful habit has been mastering you.

If you've done that, you get what Olivia said.

> OLIVIA
>
> Every morning, I wake up. And I
> promise myself. I won't use today.
> I'll detox. I'll resist. Then the
> twitching starts. The dry heaves,
> chills. So I give in. All over
> again. You think I want this? Any
> of it? I don't. But it's no use. I
> can't stop.

If you struggle with an addiction or harmful behavior like Olivia, know that you're not alone. The best of us have been there. The Apostle Paul openly confessed his personal struggle to master sin in this next passage.

For what I am doing, I do not understand; for I am not practicing what I would like to do, but I am doing the very thing I hate… 24 *Wretched man that I am!*

—Romans 7:15, 24a

Remember my convertible joyride debacle? All the way home, I was anything but joyful. Instead, I kept bludgeoning myself. Why did I do that? How could I face my dear mom after breaking my word to her? I wasn't familiar with Paul's passage in Romans, but that's exactly what I was feeling.

When I got home, I blubbered out the whole rotten escapade to my mother. How had I turned into this terrible excuse for a human being? I couldn't understand why I kept doing things like that. I hated myself for disappointing Mom and Dad again. How could I ever expect Mom to trust me now, when I couldn't even trust myself?

If you're at a loss to beat a harmful pattern in your life, like I was, you know firsthand what Paul was talking about in Romans 7:15. You get how impossible it can seem to master these damaging, controlling behaviors. It feels like a vicious cycle with no way out. You beat yourself down until there's nowhere to look but up. You cry out like Paul did.

Who will set me free from the body of this death? 25 *Thanks be to God through Jesus Christ our Lord!*

—Romans 7:24b–25a

How About You?

I know it can be hard to admit these things, even to yourself. But quietly identifying what may be controlling you—that's a brave first step to take. It's a truth that can help set you free (John 8:32).

- Have you developed a pattern of substance abuse?

- Are you hiding any type of harmful behavior?

If anything came to mind there, know that you have God's compassion. And you've just taken a giant step into His tender care by recognizing your struggle honestly.

What's an Addict's Loved One to Do?

As people like McKenna and Olivia's sister Lily found, addicts of all stripes have ancillary victims: the people who love them. Armchair advice seems easy to dole out until addiction strikes you and your family.

If you're clean yourself, you feel the raw, unmedicated pain of estrangement—and the uncertainty if that prodigal you love will ever truly come home to you. You're used to walking on eggshells about how to best communicate.

Our Lily, actress Ariane Ireland, shared these thoughts.

"You have your judgments about someone who could allow themselves to become entangled in addiction. But when you have that experience yourself and you see how easy it can be and how much of a human [Olivia] is—you know, it's hard. That relationship shows a lot of the hardship and tension. Like, 'I don't know who you are anymore.' And—reconciliation—it's something you want for everybody."

—Ariane Ireland (Lily)

Anyone who's been there, like Lily and McKenna, knows how hard it can be to right the communication ship once it's capsized. This is especially true if—in the heat of emotional outbursts—hurtful things slammed doors between us.

You know how it is. You're prayed up. Maybe you're feeling pumped by how you've just helped somebody else. That's how McKenna would have felt coming home, riding the high of aiding Courier Jacob in helping Olivia.

If you recall, after that, McKenna climbed her porch steps, then gazed at her *Truth* stone. With great resolve, she said, "Let's do this."

"Do what?" you may ask. "Who does her *let's* refer to?"

In that moment, McKenna decided that she was ready to finally have an honest conversation with her father. She knew it would be hard, given her dad's opinion that her mother's interactive faith was delusional. So she said, "Let's do this" to enlist God's presence. Surely, He'd help her come clean with her dad about her own growing faith, right?

So how did things go so horribly awry?

Dopamine. And its sidekick Adrenaline.

Spirit-Led vs Chemically Controlled

Have you ever noticed how challenging it can be to tell the difference between dopamine-fueled human resolve and Spirit-inspired conviction? I have.

Gratefully, the Holy Spirit has an app for that.

It's a spiritual gift that all believers should seek, called *distinguishing of spirits* (1 Corinthians 12:10). This much-needed gift is about far more than just discerning evil spirits. In part, this gift is there to help us distinguish whether we're being driven by our own determination or truly led by the Holy Spirit. God also uses this gift to show us the state of other people's human spirits.

Can you see how incredibly valuable discernment can be in navigating relationships?

Discernment helps us recognize what kind of spirit is at work in others. God uses it to show us if that person's human spirit is ready to hear what we have to say—or if it's better to wait for a more opportune moment to stage that longed-for intervention event.

> *There is an appointed time for everything. And there is a time for every event under heaven.*
>
> —Ecclesiastes 3:1

Granted, it can be challenging to distinguish between the Holy Spirit's leading and our own heart's desires—especially when we're fired up to do something that seems so good, like telling the truth. Still, it's best to pause and discern what God may have to say about the best time to do that good thing.

Like McKenna, our intentions may be pure. But when we're driving on dopamine, it's easy to miss the Spirit's stop signs. For McKenna, finding her father passed out drunk on the sofa should have been a flashing red signpost.

This was not the right timing.

But by then, her adrenaline was already surging. Though McKenna felt completely justified about venting her outrage about the missing Bibles, her emotions were running way hot. Her drunken dad was a powder keg too.

Rusty Joiner had this to say about how his character Andrew reacted in his grief-stricken state:

"He's just hurt. And when we hurt, we lash out."
—Rusty Joiner (Andrew)

Still, as much as Andrew lashed out—who drew blood first? McKenna. Overwhelmed by anger, she took on the role of accuser. Sure, everything McKenna said was true. But it wasn't the right timing. And her words didn't have the Spirit-led maturity of the truth spoken in love.

...but speaking the truth in love, we are to grow up in all aspects into Him who is the head, even Christ.
—Ephesians 4:15

I don't know about you. But when conflict erupts, controlling my spirit enough to sense the leading of the Holy Spirit has been one of life's great challenges. I'll admit I've failed. And still do. But with God's help, I've also seen far more issues resolved when the truth is spoken in love.

This means resisting all brain chemistry-fueled anger. It means filtering out those snippy, retaliatory comebacks that throw gas on the fire. It requires actively communing with the Spirit amid any conflict. It means surrendering that natural urge to engage in that war of words.

It's also one of the dearest ways God has demonstrated His protective love and guiding presence to me.

Thank God, the more we exercise the Holy Spirit's fruit of self-control in the real time of human conflict, the stronger that spiritual muscle grows. And the more room we give the Spirit to work through us on behalf of our relationships.

If you've been there too, you know what I mean.

As I think back on my truncated joyride at 16, I realize that this kind of godly restraint was first demonstrated to me by my mother. I marvel at the Spirit-led way she responded to me when I got home, fresh off breaking my word to her.

My Moment of Truth

That joyride night wasn't my "come to Jesus" moment. It was more about coming to the end of myself.

Actually, I was stunned at how my mother reacted when I got home in such a hot mess. She didn't say much. Quietly, she just listened while I dumped out the vile contents of my self-loathing heart.

In that moment, a strangely comforting realization came over me. Mom seemed to get how deeply sorry I was. She didn't scold or condemn me—not when she could see that I was already condemning myself.

There we were, right after I'd completely broken my word to her. And she believed me. Though we never talked about it, I'm convinced she saw the work God was doing in my heart. She sensed the crossroads of faith I'd come to in His perfect timing.

Even then, she didn't push ahead of what the Holy Spirit was doing. She just loved me. She quietly gave me grace.

Not many weeks later, when I finally went all-in with Jesus, Mom got the answer to her most fervent prayers for me. And since that day, it's been the greatest joy of my life to follow the way of Truth that my Lord Jesus is. Mercifully,

He's recreated me into His image—as the woman of my word that I so desperately wanted to be.

Trial and Error

Maybe you've tried to have an honest conversation with someone in your life. It could have blown up in a flashfire of brain chemistry, like it did for McKenna. Somehow, despite your best intentions, things went from bad to worse.

Take heart.

In our story, McKenna and her father parted in the worst possible way. Jagged emotional wounds were ripped open and left hemorrhaging. Andrew didn't have the "come to Jesus" moment McKenna wanted for him. Far from it.

Instead. Andrew's grief erupted into a deluge of painful memories that tortured him about how he'd failed both McKenna and his beloved, late wife. Why hadn't he stopped Eliana on that tragic day? How could he possibly live with himself?

In the heat of those emotionally charged exchanges between father and daughter, it seemed they'd both crossed the point of no return.

Yet 1.5 isn't the last episode. Their story continues.

And so can yours. As long as you and that loved one have breath, your story isn't over either.

God of Abraham, Isaac, and Jacob—and my Abba Father, thank You for never giving up on me. Help me to live truthfully with You and the people You've given me to love.

Fill me with Your Holy Spirit's patience, grace, and compassion—especially for those who suffer with addictions beyond their control. Above all, help me forgive and love the way You do, in Jesus' name.

DISCUSSION QUESTIONS

apply

—————◆●◆—————

1. What struggles or challenges did you relate to most in this episode?

2. Mooch a little humble pie off our Courier Jacob. Have you ever colluded, manipulated the truth, lied, or broken your word to get your way or something you felt entitled to have? If you haven't already, confess now and ask the Lord for forgiveness. Is there anything you can do now to make things right with anyone you've wronged?

ADDITIONAL NOTES

3. In our story, relationship-wary McKenna tests the waters with Tanner by telling him something that casts her in a less than positive light.

    a) In new friendships, do you tend to admit your personal fails? Why or why not?

    b) How can you make others feel safe and best honor their trust when they confide hard truths with you?

4. Is there anyone you've been reluctant to tell the truth to about your relationship with God? If so, what has stopped you from having that honest conversation?

ADDITIONAL NOTES

ACTIVATIONS

Some activations, such as this one, can involve optional levels depending on how deep you decide to venture into them. Consider these three levels of commitment to the three-in-one activation below.

Go to a Meeting

Whether you're an addict or not, go to an addict's or addict's family support group (whichever is appropriate given your status as an addict or the loved one of an addict). Go for yourself or go in support of a loved one. Even if you don't know anyone, go to increase your understanding for what addicts and their loved ones are going through.

Make a Friend

Within the anonymity of that support group, identify someone to pray for and see regularly there. Greet that new friend warmly at each meeting. (Be sure to respect and honor their confidentiality policies.)

Practice God's Presence

No matter what you're doing or who's there with you, practice connecting with God amid any human interaction. Resist the urge to talk about yourself much. Instead, ask the Holy Spirit to give you ears to take interest in the other person. Listen for any words of encouragement, truth, and life He gives you to speak into that person you've befriended.

Episode 1.6

forgiven

---•---

Be kind to one another, tender-hearted, forgiving each other,
just as God in Christ also has forgiven you.

—Ephesians 4:32

What is your first impulse when a conversation with a loved one completely blows up, right in your face? Honestly, in the flashfire of that instant, something inside begs me to run away. I want to distance myself from whoever just hurt or disrespected me. My impulse is to ditch that person and lick my wounds.

Like McKenna did.

For McKenna, it didn't matter that sleeping on the stock room table wasn't as comfy as her bed at home. She just knew she felt safer there. Away from her dad. Miles from her mom's prayer closet and any direction she might get there.

So McKenna bolted. She responded to her natural brain chemistry—as we're all predisposed to do.

Though McKenna is our beloved heroine, she's flawed. Still, mistakes can be her best teachers. This one leaves her waking up stiff and crabby. She's canceling everything— including her dad, her inherited home, and the Program. Of her own choice, she's become a lost sheep. She's separated herself from the fold.

Would you blame her?

Probably not—because you've been there yourself.

And so have I.

In the heat of such emotionally charged moments, our first instinct is self-preservation. We don't think. We don't pray. We don't count the cost. We do what comes naturally.

We fight back and/or run.

But the Bible says there's a better way.

Abba Knows Best

Even if you know this next passage virtually by heart, read it again with your own conflict dynamics in mind.

> *But earnestly desire the greater gifts. And I show you a still more excellent way... Love is patient, love is kind and is not jealous; love does not brag and is not arrogant, 5 does not act unbecomingly; it does not seek its own, is not provoked, does not take into account a wrong suffered, 6 does not rejoice in unrighteousness, but rejoices with the truth; 7 bears all things, believes all things, hopes all things, endures all things. 8 Love never fails...*
>
> —1 Corinthians 12:31, 13:4–8a

It's interesting that this more *"excellent way"* love passage follows Paul's urging to earnestly desire the greater gifts—all of which require lovingly interacting with God and others in the Spirit. This is the same Holy Spirit who supplies all the emotion-stabilizing fruit we need to wisely navigate conflict.

> *But the fruit of the Spirit is love, joy, peace, patience, kindness, goodness, faithfulness,* 22 *gentleness, self-control, against such things there is no law.*
>
> —Galatians 5:22–23

Sure, responding to conflict in the Spirit doesn't come naturally. Reacting in the brain chemistry of our flesh does. But responding in the Holy Spirit is the secret sauce of renewing relationships.

Many deem spiritual gifts such as prophecy, healing, or working of miracles to be among the greater gifts that Paul mentioned. But let's not forget how speaking Spirit-led words in love can heal our relationships and the miracle that reconciliation can be.

A Spiritual Chem Lab Experiment

Days before I wrote this, someone said something harsh to me—seemingly out of nowhere. Granted, it was nothing compared to McKenna's verbal brawl with her dad. Still, I could feel that adrenaline fueled "fight or flight" drive kick in (the one we talked about in the last chapter).

True confession. One snarky barb and my first natural instinct was to either fight back or get away from that person who'd snapped at me.

In the heat of that moment, I ran a real-time experiment. I volunteered to be a spiritual lab rat.

I didn't bolt. Instead, I took a breath—drawing from the self-control of the Spirit. That adrenaline rush kept prickling at first, coaxing me to bark back (fight) or bolt (flight). But as I quietly kept breathing, a funny thing happened. I could feel the adrenaline start to dissipate. Sure enough, not a minute passed before that natural urge to bark or bolt subsided.

Now, I'm far from perfect.

But when convos veer south like that, I try to make connecting with God my go-to response—right in the thick of that moment. Whether or not I've felt wronged, or a boundary needs to be drawn, taking in the breath of God always helps me. Immediately. He opens my eyes to see what He's doing. He opens my ears to hear how best to diffuse that conflict, rather than escalate it.

Just that momentary prayer-pause gives my natural brain chemistry a chance to settle down. This makes it far easier to navigate any relational aftermath in the better way of love.

How About You?

Spend a moment taking your spiritual temperature when it comes to navigating conflict.

- Are you more likely to fight back or flee?

- Is it harder to hold your tongue or your horses?

- Are you willing to try God's better way in real time?

Snatched in the Spirit

Of course, with respect to McKenna's blowout with her dad, McKenna's tale is a cautionary one. In the aftermath, we find her sheepish heart, dodging texts from Central Dispatch. She shuffles to the Thrift Store bathroom for a shower, far from her mom's prayer closet portal.

This lost sheep forgets her Shepherd tracks with her.

As we all tend to forget.

Of course, it doesn't occur to McKenna that the Spirit can scoop her up and snatch her away from anywhere (Acts 8:39). Yet as abruptly as McKenna is brought back to the fold, she's still given a free-will choice.

Just like you and I get.

If you've been there, you know the deeper and dirtier the wounds are that brought you to that disenfranchised place, the more sensitive you are in that area. And the gentler you hope your Great Physician and His emissaries will be about lancing and cleaning those wounds for you.

You know that kind of spiritual surgery requires going back. It makes you revisit the painful chain of events that got you into that mess. You know firsthand that sometimes, it's like cracking your spiritual chest open—to get to the heart of whatever's been tormenting you.

Life and Death in the Balance

For McKenna, spiritual surgery meant facing both times that her mother willingly risked her life for her (John 15:13). Actress Charlene Amoia recounts her thoughts on what that choice required of Eliana the first time she made it.

"Rusty—who plays Andrew—and I had to go back 20 years prior, to this moment where I'm pregnant. And I have to make this very difficult decision when we get some news from the doctor.

It was the reality of those circumstances and having to really get in contact with God. And let that be the louder voice in the decision making, rather than a medical professional or a human being who could be making a mistake. So it was a really tough decision—life and death for my character— and potentially for my baby's character."

—Charlene Amoia (Eliana)

Just like you or a loved one may have experienced, there are times when the stakes are literally life and death. These are the times we get most desperate for answers.

Loved ones disagree about the best course. We wrestle with human fears and opinions. Even the finest doctors can only cite odds of survival given one choice versus another. They can't say for sure. With life hanging in the balance, we can't afford to get it wrong.

So we cry out in earnest.

"Please, God," we say. "I'm begging You. Tell me. What should I do?"

In our story, Eliana relied on the promise of God, given in a dream to her mother, Louise. At the risk of her own safety, she chose life for the child growing inside her. She responded to Andrew's fear in faith, fully aware that her life was on the line.

Facing Crossroads with God

When we stare down these life-or-death crossroads with God, it feels scary. His words can pierce us—like the *Courage* stone Eliana had recently received in our story. Try as she might, Eliana found it even harder to be brave after Miriam confirmed what she'd already discerned.

McKenna faced grave danger that day.

You know how it is at perilous crossroads. We want to know exactly how that trial or that risk we're taking will play out in real time. We long for God to dictate details we think we need to navigate those trying times best.

Deep down, we hope God will spare us very the trials Jesus said we'd face in life. But ultimately, every crossroads means picking up a cross. Every choice means dying to other choices with other potential outcomes.

The truth is exactly as Jesus put it. Tough times go with the territory we travel in life, just as they did for Him. The Lord doesn't exempt us from trials. Instead, He speaks peace to our troubled hearts.

> *These things I have spoken to you, so that in Me you may have peace. In the world you have tribulation, but take courage, I have overcome the world.*
>
> —John16:33

As you face your crossroads, you may feel as alarmed as Eliana became. Hearing "take courage" might amp up your desperation to hear more. But the Holy Spirit is not a fortune teller. And as much as God asks us to trust what He tells us, He also wants us to trust Him in the mystery of what we're not told—or what we're only told in part.

For we know in part, and we prophesy in part.
—1 Corinthians 13:9

Often, hearing from God requires us to live out the uncertainty of those crossroads in faith, as Eliana explained in these script lines below.

ELIANA
I mean, it's not like we see the whole picture. We get pieces.
High stakes choices to live out, in the moment of whatever unfolds.

These are the kinds of choices my old roommate from college faced after two brutal rounds of chemo—and the choice to try another course or to leave her healing in God's hands. It's one of the times she heard from Him most tenderly and clearly. But only in part. He would require her to trust Him and make that crossroads decision in faith.

"I am going to bring your suffering to an end," He said.

When she shared this with me, I remember my friend explaining that she wasn't sure what God's words meant. Would He heal her in this life or the next? Either way, she was grateful and at peace with His promise.

Soon, updated scans showed that she'd gone into full remission. Though friends and family celebrated and declared complete healing, it was news I took in soberly.

As dearly as I loved her, I wanted to believe she'd been healed like others I've seen miraculously healed before. But that's when that still, small voice came to me. God confided that this remission would only be a temporary relief—a time to get her house in order and love on her family. After a short reprieve, He would receive her into His healing arms forever.

Rightly Dividing the Word of Truth

It seems there will always be those who misinterpret God's Word to suit human hopes and persuasions. They say that if we only had enough faith, things would always go as hoped. We'd always be healed in this life. But when we read the whole Bible in context, another empowered outworking of the Holy Spirit emerges. Faith.

We see Jesus heading boldly into Jerusalem, knowing the horrific death He'd face for us there. We read how Paul—even after receiving repeated prophetic words that suffering and chains awaited him in Jerusalem—followed the leading of the Spirit. Paul went into that threatening place, willing to be bound or die for the name of his Savior (Acts 21:8–13).

As we mature in hearing God's voice, we come to that place of acceptance that my old roommate did. We long to hear from Him, no matter what He has to say.

Like Eliana, we face that the *Courage* word we just got isn't only for somebody else. It's a word God meant for us to live into as well.

In these crossroads moments, even the spiritually mature may tremble, as Eliana does in our story. Like Paul, we may weigh words of wisdom we've received in light of the pivotal choice set before us. We may ask God to let that bitter cup pass from us. The bravest of us entrust ourselves to the will of God as Jesus did. Then we set our faces like flint. And we move toward our Jerusalem in faith, even if that means laying down our lives.

How About You?

Think of any significant crossroads decisions that you've faced in the past or are facing currently.

- Does difficulty or suffering tend to threaten or increase your faith? How so?

- Have you ever sensed the Holy Spirit moving you to sacrificially lay down your time, treasure, or life for the sake of His name or for someone you love?

Picking up Your Cross

In the aftermath of loss or suffering, we go through stages of grief. We wrestle with denial, anger, bargaining, and depression. Some of us never get to acceptance. Our souls get too tangled in knots over those first four stages.

If you've been there, you get it.

Your mind circles the hamster wheel, relentlessly trying to figure out why it had to happen and who's at fault. As with McKenna, you might blame or shame yourself (or others). "If onlys" taunt incessantly. Though God may have forgiven you, you may find it impossible to believe that.

Because you haven't forgiven yourself.

Our McKenna, actress Madeline Carroll, gets that very human struggle.

"We all have that one thing. That deep hidden, whatever it is. Hurt or anger or bitterness. And it's sort of lifted to the surface for McKenna. Anybody that's watching might be dealing with something—their own hurt, their own bitterness, their own feelings."

—Madeline Carroll (McKenna)

Regret seems unique to each person. Who else thinks or feels exactly what we do amid regret's torment? Maybe we can't fathom how a loving God could allow such evil or suffering. We might wonder how anyone could understand the depth of our sorrow, shame, and weakness.

The fact is, only someone who's been there can.

Like Jesus—who died for us.

For we do not have a high priest who cannot sympathize with our weaknesses, but One who has been tempted in all things as we are, yet without sin. 16 Therefore let us draw near with confidence to the throne of grace, so that we may receive mercy and find grace to help in time of need.

—Hebrews 4:15–16

In our allegory, McKenna's need for help overwhelms her. For months, she's had far more questions than answers. She needs someone to come alongside her, like Miriam does. Then, when McKenna begs to know why her mother had to die in her place, consider how Miriam responds.

MIRIAM
Sometimes an innocent has to
die, so other people can live.

153

Though the stories in *These Stones* are fictional, Miriam's words couldn't be more true.

Jesus is that ultimate Innocent.

He understands all your struggles, your weaknesses, and your heart like no one else can. In the deepest expression of forgiveness, acceptance, and love—Jesus willingly laid down His life for the whole world.

Including you.

The Lord sacrificed Himself to bring all who would receive Him into the family of God. He sets you apart as a living stone among the household of faith. He assures you that no matter where you are or what you may fear—you can rely on His promise:

You are never alone.

You have the Bible—teaming with the true stories of people that can still speak into your life today. Literally everything you need to know is there at your fingertips. The Holy Spirit is with you—to deliver God's words to and through you. The Hosts of Heaven join with the earthly family of God to guard, encourage, and support you.

Jesus is with you. Always.

But your journey doesn't end there. It doesn't conclude with this study. When you're called according to God's purposes, each day you wake is a new beginning.

Like McKenna, every day presents opportunities—to love God and everyone He puts into your path. Like the stones of Season One, stone builds upon stone. Every word from His mouth heightens your potential to live as the multi-faceted gem He created you to become.

You connect with God when you **Listen** to His voice. You **Grow** by following His direction. You mature to **Accept** His sovereign will. You give more **Grace** to others, knowing the grace you've received yourself. You're set free to live in **Truth**. He gives you the **Courage** you need to walk by faith. And as you realize how completely **Forgiven** you are—the peace that passes understanding settles your heart.

In closing, I'll pose Scripture's question once more.

What do these stones mean?

To those who have ears to hear—they mean everything. If that's you, they mean you are cherished beyond rubies. They mean the Lover of Your Soul wants to spend time with you. And He's there to walk you down that glorious aisle of faith—into the greatest romance of all time.

———◆———

Precious Father, thank You for sending Your innocent Son to die for me. Thank You for understanding me, forgiving me, and adopting me into Your family.

Right now, in Jesus' name, I'm asking You to clothe me in the power of the Holy Spirit. Equip and anoint me afresh. Help me to love You and others with all my heart, my mind, my soul, and my strength. And may Your Kingdom come through me today.

DISCUSSION QUESTIONS

apply

1. What struggles or challenges did you relate to most in this episode?

2. Nibble on some humble pie with Miriam. Have you ever let jealousy tempt you to gossip or back-bite against a spiritual brother, sister, or authority figure? If so, take this opportunity to repent. Ask the Holy Spirit to remind you to guard against gossip in the future.

ADDITIONAL NOTES

3. Has hardship ever left you angry or bitter with God or yourself? If so, how have you dealt with that?

4. Is there anyone you wouldn't hesitate to die for? Who is that and why?

5. In light of the Bible's directive to forgive as we've been forgiven, ask yourself:

    a. Is there anyone I can't seem to forgive?

    b. Do I find it difficult to forgive myself?

    c. Is it hard to believe God has forgiven me? If so, why?

ADDITIONAL NOTES

ACTIVATIONS

Schedule Spiritual Open-Heart Surgery

Ready to clean out an old wound? Brave up and follow these steps to inner healing:

- Make an appointment with a trained and trusted prayer counselor to open an old wound before the Lord together.
- Pour out your heart.
- Ask your heavenly Father to show you where any roots of bitterness started.
- Share what God shows you with your counselor.
- Ask the Holy Spirit to show you where Jesus was with you in that picture. Describe what you see.
- Trust your Great Physician to clean out that deep wound completely.
- Forgive just as God has forgiven you.
- Listen for any words of comfort, healing, and encouragement the Spirit may give to you or your counselor.
- Turn on some healing praise music and sing with abandon.

BONUS INTERVIEWS

converse

———◆●◆———

We hope you'll enjoy this BTS (Behind-the-Scenes) peek into the making of the first season of *These Stones*. It'll give you an inside glimpse into the heart behind the series and the team that prepared it for you.

Interviews with cast and crew members were conducted on location by producers as BTS videos during production, to help support, promote, and raise awareness about *These Stones* in various ways (like this Study Guide book, for example).

Those fuller, lengthy, recorded convos our cast and crew contributed covered a variety of topics, such as why they chose to get involved with the series, what it means to them, and how they view the show's biblical themes. To follow are trimmed excerpts, drawn from some of those interviews.

Madeline Carroll (Lead Actress: McKenna)

Interviewer:

How did you get involved with the series, *These Stones?*

Madeline:

[Cheryl] texted me: "Hey, I wrote this thing. Would you be interested in it?" I obviously was going to say "yes" because she's amazing. But it's funny.

A couple of years prior, I got prayed on and this woman that prayed on me told me that when I was 26 years old, somebody was going to come to me with a story that had been written with me in mind. So, it came together and was just unbelievable. It's very divine and meant to be that I'm here.

Interviewer:

Talk about your character, McKenna.

Madeline:

McKenna is dealing with a lot of stuff that everyone can relate to on their own level. But for her personally, she has a lot going on with her dad. She is dealing with the loss of her mom. She's dealing with her own faith. She's dealing with being in trouble.

She has a lot going on that I can empathize with. We are on very different journeys. But I'm just excited to be someone that girls can look up to.

Interviewer:

What do you think sets *These Stones* apart from other shows?

Madeline:

We're bringing real-life biblical characters to the present. We've seen beautiful representations of the Bible and we've seen beautiful representations of people struggling with everyday life. But we've never seen the two collide. That's what really sets us apart.

Interviewer:

How will *These Stones* help people understand the Bible?

Madeline:

I think it's going to be helpful for people who want to discover their faith or go on a faith journey because a lot of people don't really understand the Bible. [It] can be a very intimidating thing. With *These Stones*, I'm hoping the average person that maybe never picked up a Bible in their life would be able to [say], "That's what they mean when they say that." And it's able to be broken down for them, for people of faith and people who are just entering into that journey.

I think that what's so special, too, is it's accessible to all ages. Something everybody can enjoy as a family. And so hopefully, we're giving people a key, a way of getting out. That's what I really hope comes across with *These Stones*, is we're giving people the ingredients that they need to come out the other side okay.

It just makes it "every day real" because that's how God is. God is involved in all of our lives. The fact that we have breath is from the Lord and so I'm just excited for people to experience it in a whole new way and maybe be open to things that they weren't open to before.

Charlene Amoia (Lead Actress: Eliana)

Interviewer:

What can you share about your character, Eliana, McKenna's mom?

Charlene:

I think she's the conscience of the series. I think the relationship between her and McKenna is a lot of the heartbeat. It propels McKenna's storyline forward and gets her direction on the right track because of the incidents that happen in Season One. I feel like she's a bit of an angelic voice along the way, as McKenna is making her decisions through life.

Interviewer:

What do you want viewers to get out of watching *These Stones*?

Charlene:

Hope. I certainly believe in miracles. I believe that with God, anything is possible. I think there are enough stories out there to prove that. We could always use a little bit more hope in the world in our day-to-day as life gets tough and just get back in [God's] presence and knowing that we're being looked out for.

Interviewer:

How do you hope this series helps others get to know or understand Bible stories better?

Charlene:

It brings biblical stories and characters to current day circumstances and hardships in a way that is relatable and interesting and dynamic, which is wonderful. Because sometimes when people are reading through the Bible, they can't understand—or it's not speaking to them.

So this is just a way to get to know these stories, these characters, these values in a way that we can relate to in our personal lives. There is this wonderful element in this series of the portal to this supernatural realm and how accessible it really is.

Rusty Joiner (Lead Actor: Andrew)

Interviewer:

What is your perfect Sunday afternoon?

Rusty:

I'm one of those weird guys that likes to get up at 4:30. Sunday is one of those days I spend a little more quiet-time with the morning. My perfect Sunday before worship is family time.

I grew up without a dad, [with] a single mom. And so my whole life I thought, "When I become a dad, when I get a chance, this is what I'm going to do." Because I dreamt of walking in the kitchen and smelling pancakes and everyone gathered together. No matter who eats them, we make pancakes or French toast every Saturday, every Sunday. And most of the time it's just a chaotic mess. So that for me is the start to the perfect Sunday.

Interviewer:

What drew you to want to play the role of Andrew?

Rusty:

Reading these episodes. First is knowing the concept of the show and how much loss was there. It's a beautiful story of just trying to navigate our way through life. Everything [Andrew is] going through, he never really loses his sense of being a good man.

We don't know what tomorrow brings. But we know it's heavy. And we have to go through it to get to some sort of resolution or peace on the other side. But knowing there is redemption and healing somewhere.

Interviewer:

How do you hope viewers relate to *These Stones?*

Rusty:

I think it's a wonderful, faith-based, family-friendly series that has the feel and texture of real life.

The fact that these people are a mess and life isn't perfect for them—I think it will make it so relatable to people. Because a lot of the time, there are estranged relationships between parents and children. This story for me is about extreme loss, devastation, but knowing somehow, someway, there's good in it. There's God in it and healing.

Karen Abercrombie (Lead Actress: Miriam)

Interviewer:

Many know you as Miss Clara in *War Room*. We were thankful you signed on to play a Bible character for us. How did you get involved in *These Stones*?

Karen:

I always say I want to be in [God's] will. Out of His way. And so, I just trust, do my part, try to be as ready as I can and then open up to allow Him to flow.

One of the writers is a friend of mine, Cheryl. She told me about the project, asked what I thought about it. I was like, "This is fresh. This is exciting. I love the strategy, the approach. Yes, I would love to be a part of this." And so here I am. Grateful to be.

Interviewer:

How do you see the biblical concepts in *These Stones*?

Karen:

It's a brilliant, incredible strategy, right on time. It's the story as old as time, literally. The way it is put together teaches without hitting anybody over the head with the Bible. Because as soon as you do that, they tune out. And even people that are believers have heard it before. It's exciting and it's ancient. It would be intriguing for just about anyone. I would say teens on up. It is absolutely captivating and fresh.

Cameron Arnett (Recurring Guest Star: Aaron)

Interviewer:

Tell us about the Bible character you play—Aaron, Moses' brother.

Cameron:

Aaron is an extremely interesting character because, talking about the mouthpiece, second in line, but also, he messed up. So you have this "what if" situation now that he's still living. All these characters are living. What would that be like?

And I think for [Aaron], he's a very grateful man, on this side of things, on the other side of Christ and everything else. But then to know the forgiveness, the love of God on this end. How thankful that in spite of his past, he's forgiven. He's accepted.

Interviewer:

How did you get involved in *These Stones*?

Cameron:

[Cheryl & I] have worked together before. And when she started telling me about the story, of course, I was like, "Oh, man, this is great." Again, that "what if" perspective and the intricacies of "what if" these kind of things could happen in the story, develop out of it? It was kind of like a no-brainer, in a sense of wanting to do it. I'm just fortunate that I get an opportunity.

Interviewer:

What kind of impact do you hope *These Stones* has?

Cameron:

I think it's going to have a great impact because, you know, I really think people are tired of having no choices, no options. They're tired of being led astray or being pulled into a direction [with movies] that they don't want to take their family.

I think whether you are Christian or whether you're someone who doesn't know God yet, there's a piece in there for you. People will be able to look at the characters—those that are in the "what if" situation, but also those that are being helped—and see themselves, their need, and see where they fit in, where they want to fit and how they can actually change things.

Interviewer:

What would you want to tell viewers about the show?

Cameron:

I want to tell viewers is that God is in love with you and it really doesn't matter where you've been, what you've done, what you've gone through. Don't believe the lie that God will not receive you if you would come to Him. He sent His son, Jesus Christ, just for you.

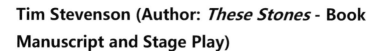

Tim Stevenson (Author: *These Stones* - Book Manuscript and Stage Play)

Interviewer:

Tells us about the Scripture reference that became your inspiration for the stage play, *These Stones*.

Tim:

There's a passage in Matthew 27 that says when Jesus died, three things happened. The great earthquake, the temple curtain split in two, and the Holy Ones came out of their graves and went into the city. That passage has always amazed me, and I thought, "What a great play that would be." So, what if those people are still around? The Bible never says what happened to them. What if they're still here?

Interviewer:

How did you develop the "what if" of those verses?

Tim:

What started as a play turned into a book and now turned into a television series, which is pretty awesome. To see that hope people can have that the Scriptures are true and that's what *These Stones* can do.

Interviewer:

What is your greatest hope for this series?

Tim:

My greatest hope is that people will see. The spark will happen inside of them to maybe investigate further. Maybe look up some of the characters that are being talked about in *These Stones.* That it will lead them to realize there is a God who loves them. Jesus will give them hope in their life. We're not over here for eternity.

Interview:

How did you work with your co-author Peggy Porter, once you shifted from a play to a novel?

Tim:

[Peggy] started getting really involved in it, really excited about the story, suggesting different things, and correcting my bad grammar. Every time I'd go out in my courtyard and start typing, I'd send her the next chapter or two, and she'd read it and give suggestions.

It's been really fun to be with my prayer partner. She's an amazing lady.

Interviewer:

Any final words of encouragement?

Tim:

I would just say to encourage people that God is real, and God does give dreams, God gives visions. Dreams don't chase after you. You've got to chase after them.

Peggy Porter (Co-Author: *These Stones* - Book Manuscript)

Interviewer:

What inspired you to get involved in Tim's book project, *These Stones?*

Peggy:

Tim was working on a play for an Easter program and asked me to come alongside. I love how Tim writes and eagerly accepted. What started out on my part as editing soon became writing as well. The play grew too large to be an Easter program and turned into a book.

Interviewer:

How do you apply the Bible to your life today?

Peggy:

Coming from a background where I was not allowed to have a Bible or attend church, my Bible and the freedom to own it is a privilege I never take for granted. My Bible is my letter straight from my Lord to me to teach and train me.

Interviewer:

What are your hopes for the TV series version of *These Stones?*

Peggy:

My hope and prayer [is] that God uses *These Stones* to reach countless people with the truth of Scripture. God cares. He loves us so much that He gave us His only Son so that whoever believes will have eternal life (John 3:16). I pray nonbelievers get inspired to pick up a Bible and begin to search out the biblical characters from each episode. I hope God uses their time in Scripture to lead them to faith in Jesus.

For the believers, I pray it is a powerful reminder that no matter what is going on in your life, God is here. You are never alone.

Jeanette Towne (Executive Producer)

Interviewer:

It's your pastor who came up with the inspiration behind *These Stones*. What caught your attention about it, to draw you to get involved in producing a TV show for the first time?

Jeanette:

[Pastor Tim] fictionalized something that came out of the Bible. And I sent it to Cheryl. I said, "Hey, I'd love for you to take a look at this piece. I think it's very cool."

Interviewer:

What inspired you to bring Bible characters into present day through this show?

Jeanette:

They were really flawed people. All of the problems today and what they went through in the past. What is so unique is we can identify with their humanity, their frailty, their sin, their carnal nature, and everything in between that they've gone through.

We go through it today. So we are taking this Scripture, and we are allegorically exploring the "what if" of it, using these Bible characters that maybe you don't know about. Maybe you do. And we're putting them into contemporary situations.

Interviewer:

What kind of storylines are you excited about?

Jeanette:

We're not shying away from opioid addiction, from losing a parent, the plight of an adult with special needs, a teenager cutting. These are things that we hear about that your families are going through now. We are using these characters that have gone through similar things, being used by God today to help people get through what they're going through.

Interviewer:

What do you hope *These Stones* can help audiences do?

Jeanette:

God only knows where it's going to go. I believe that this has innumerable opportunities to inspire, educate, and show people that God is real.

God is here today and is working miracles in the lives of people, ordinary people, every day. Just being able to be open to what God has for us to give to people and being used by God to help, to inspire, to lead, to minister to people.

Mike Burns (Executive Producer)

Interviewer:

What is the heart of *These Stones*?

Mike:

These Stones brings together the idea that we are never alone, that we constantly have people that are by our side, that have our back and that we can look towards. What's so special about it is that we believe that God is alive today and loves us. He works through ordinary people, and typically, He works through trials.

Interviewer:

What do you hope viewers will take away from Season One of *These Stones*?

Mike:

Season One has so many themes to help remind me about God in my everyday life. Thomas and Jonathan's male hurts and suffering are real. But God is there with them. Jimmy's longing for more and his mom's fear and natural desire to protect him.

Andrew's checking out and coping through booze to mask his pain and hurt. His profound love for McKenna and Eliana. His anger at God (and daughter and late wife) for taking away his "perfect" life.

Brock and Drea's waiting for their answer. Trying to remain positive and hopeful. Being reminded of God's blessing of others all around them. And when their answer finally comes, it's a complete letdown and unsatisfying in their moment.

How temptation and sin for Katie and Vince lead to counterfeit happiness, dark outcomes, and hardened hearts. And that God forgives, erases the lies, and can restore beauty from ashes when we have an open heart and mind.

Olivia being on-top of her game in the news world one day, to the lowest pits of despair and squalor just a year later. Lily's real and justified anger towards Olivia. And her God-inspired ability to forgive Olivia because deep down she loves her sister.

Miriam, McKenna, Rahab playing the devil's "woulda-coulda-shoulda" game, reminding, replaying, and kicking themselves for things that they did or didn't do. Wrestling with the idea of why a good God would allow bad stuff to happen. There are so many takeaways for today.

Interviewer:

If you could choose one biblical Courier who applies most to your life experience, who would that be and why?

Mike:

Joseph's story (son of Jacob and Rachel) illustrates elevation, resilience, faithfulness, and ultimately redemption. He was misunderstood, betrayed, and endured hardships, yet he maintained his integrity and faith in God. Joseph was given high-standing and influence. He was elevated to be the right-hand man to Potiphar and eventually to advise the Pharaoh.

In 2013, God allowed a profound shake-up in my successful business career which seemingly left no part of my life the same. My identity, how I made a living, provided for my family, and my future purpose were forever challenged and changed. I was really mad at God. I didn't like or understand how He could allow this to happen.

But the truth is, prior to this shakeup, I was really burned out, overweight and unhealthy, unhappy, and wanted a lot more meaning out of my life. I came to realize God allowed this career shakeup to get my attention. To bring forth better. Much better. Because He loved me. And sometimes better looks different.

I wish that Joseph could have visited me then...and even now. His story serves as a powerful example of someone who faced adversity, lost his way through betrayal and false accusations, but ultimately emerged successful and fulfilled God's greater plan for his life.

Interview:

How do you apply the Bible to your life today?

Mike:

I use the Bible to see what God has to say to me, today and now, or about my future and past. As I read passages and stories, He sometimes reveals profound—but more often subtle—nudges and messages to me on how what I just read applies in my life.

There's a reason the Bible is referred to as the Living Word. It is alive. My gained faith and knowledge are always growing and changing. But it's me that's being changed through His Word. God's Word and love for me remain steadfast yet are revealed in a new way every day.

Dexter Masland (Recurring Lead Actor: Tanner)

Interviewer:

How did you prepare to play the role of Tanner, a 9-1-1 Operator, in *These Stones*?

Dexter:

One of the things that I discovered through my research and preparation was—to be a 9-1-1 dispatcher—you're getting these calls every day that are pretty traumatic, that [trauma] these people are going through. Every day someone's calling, having, like, the worst experience of their life.

I actually went on YouTube and found some, and it's hard to listen. What the kids are calling in about, what they're experiencing or what this woman's calling in [about], in the middle of the situation. My instinct as "me" is to turn away and turn it off. I don't want to be upset by that. I don't want to deal with that. I want to pretend it's not real.

But Tanner, you know, moves toward that, is there for that. That's what [he's] chosen to do, as [his] profession is to receive those calls and help those people.

Interviewer:

Are there any similarities between you and Tanner?

Dexter:

There are a lot of similarities. Tanner has just started down this road, being a Christian. That's a thing I really related to. I became a Christian in college, gave my life to the Lord. So I really resonate with that.

I feel like I am just starting down this road, even though it's been probably a decade. That's something I really loved about my character was getting to bring a lot of what I've experienced to the character.

Interviewer:

How do you think *These Stones* will resonate with today's audiences?

Dexter:

I think *These Stones* will resonate with people because it's really a story about how the Bible finds you in the midst of what you're going through, how God meets you through those stories, in your story of what you're going through, your deepest heartbreak.

You see the world through McKenna, who's experienced the lowest of the lows. And in that place, God meets her.

I think that's something that provides a lot of hope—where I know for me, when I was at my lowest points, God was always there. Even though you don't necessarily feel it, He's there. I think people watching this will get a lot of hope from that.

Erin Bethea (Producer/Guest Star: Drea/Ep 1.3)

Interviewer:

What was it about *These Stones* that made you want to be a part of it?

Erin:

I was excited to participate in *These Stones*, largely because—whether a project is faith-based or not—I'm really interested in projects that authentically reflect the human experience. Some faith-based projects do that really well and some are afraid of offending people or crossing a line. So they don't always get down to the heart or the rawness of an issue.

If we don't show the pain, if we don't show the loss, if we don't show the darkness—then the light doesn't have as much power. To me, what's appealing about these kinds of projects are the ones that people are going to be able to see themselves in these characters.

That's one of the things that really appealed to me—the idea that we were really going to be digging into some tough subjects and hard things to talk about. And we see that, with Drea, she has a very relatable problem. It's a series that is not shying away from reality today.

And as an actor, my job is for people to look at me and be able to see a reflection of themselves. And I think this series is going to do that in a really powerful way.

Interviewer:

Since this episode crosses particularly sensitive ground, we'd love to dig a little deeper with you. How do you sense Drea processing her journey on subconscious and spiritual levels?

Erin:

I think the thing that happened with Drea is what happens to so many of us. She is so focused on this one goal of having children—this goal that she and her husband set together—that's a beautiful, wonderful thing that most women, I think to some degree, desire at some point in their lives. And yet she's sort of sacrificing the thing that makes that goal possible in the pursuit of it.

And I think that's a very relatable position that we find ourselves in sometimes in the pursuit of something good, in the pursuit of something right. We get so focused on that good thing that we want to do in the world that it puts blinders on us. And we miss the other things that God has for us.

We miss the relationships that He has for us. We miss the small connections, the little things, because we just feel like we have this mission or this purpose, which is important. But getting that singularly focused on it, things fall by the wayside. The reason that you have that purpose, right? If you get so focused on doing good that you forget to have relationships with others, then all the good in the world isn't really going to have accomplished anything.

Interviewer:

How did you feel about the supernatural aspects of the series?

Erin:

That's one of the things that makes *These Stones* a really unique series. For a lot of people who don't have a relationship with God—it's hard for them to understand the idea of receiving a word from God or having a personal connection with Him.

Those of us who have that relationship, we know we don't usually hear this audible voice of God. But what I like about what's been done with this series is—it's sort of putting that in a tangible way where it's like, if He wanted to, this is how He could speak to us.

And to some degree, it's a reminder to us that He does send people into our lives to speak wisdom from their experiences. And they may not be a Bible character traveling through a time portal. But that doesn't mean they're any less designated by God for that moment and that season in our lives. And that is one of the ways that we hear from Him— through others in our lives who speak into our circumstances.

Micah Lynn Hanson (Guest Star: Sarah/Ep 1.3)

Interviewer:

You play a Courier in our show. A Bible character who is still here, Abraham's wife Sarah. How was that for you?

Micah:

It's just a thrill to get to play a biblical character. To have grown up with these people, learning about them, so much from them and from their stories. It's really beautiful to get to bring one of them to the screen.

Interviewer:

What do you hope viewers will get when they experience the stories in *These Stones*?

Micah:

I think everybody has a different biblical character that they may really resonate with. It's beautiful how it's kind of like a modern twist on how God uses [them], how the Word is alive, and how it ministers to different people.

So particularly, God can use the same words on the page that I've read a million times. I'll read it when I'm going through something else. Or maybe I'm just going to open my Bible today and read a verse before I go off on my day and it's like, "Wow, I never realized that before." So, I think that's kind of a fun, different twist on this. How the Word can come to life and minister to somebody's soul.

Interviewer:

Your episode talks about how, while miracles exist, they are not the normal course of day-to-day life. Can you talk about the role of miracles in your life?

Micah:

I've experienced miracles in my life. I'm a walking miracle. I should have died a couple of times, quite honestly. God has done amazing things in my life, and I know miracles happen every single day.

I hope that other people can see this and maybe start seeing the little miracles in their lives that you don't notice sometimes—like God is always working.

Sometimes, we're not looking for it. Sometimes, we just don't have the eyes and the ears to see and hear what He's doing. But just because we don't see it, doesn't mean He's not moving.

Interviewer:

When playing the role of Sarah, what impact did she have on your life?

Micah:

[Sarah] has given me a lot of hope. I think it was a really good reminder for me to see how badly somebody [else] screwed up and to know that God still loves them and has the best at heart for them. That it's not about your performance. Like when things don't happen the way that you think they should.

When you go through hard things, it's not that you deserved it. It's not that you did something to earn that. It's that God still has your absolute best at heart, even when your life looks nothing like you thought it should.

My life looks nothing like I planned it out or wanted it to look like. But it really is better. When you allow yourself to learn the lesson, then you truly see it. I am a firm believer that everything happens *for* you, not to you. I know that my God will work everything out for good if I allow Him to.

If I choose to see [life with] myself as a victim, I'll be the victim forever. I choose to see it as, "God allowed this in my life. He loves me. This is good for me because He's allowed it."

Katherine Shepler (Guest Star: Katie/Ep 1.4)

Interviewer:

You play our troubled teenager, a cutter who has issues with self-harm and self-loathing. What drew you to play Katie?

Katherine:

Her desire to be vulnerable. She has such a tender heart, and she unfortunately allows people to abuse that. And over time, it becomes hardened. But she still has this desire to be vulnerable and this desire to be soft, which is ultimately why she seeks help. She seeks hope. She's drawn towards that.

She doesn't close off completely. I think that's really important. An amazing message for a lot of young women her age is, "It's okay to be vulnerable. And it's okay to open up and ask for help as well." I love that she's willing to do that.

Interviewer:

How does trying to be perfect affect Katie?

Katherine:

She ends up self-harming as a result of that pressure. So it clearly is intense enough that she feels like she has to get out some sort of energy and tension in some way.

I think the pressure to be perfect is really heavy because it's impossible to be perfect. So you have a standard of perfection, either put on you by [others or] yourself, which is mainly what Katie has. It is this self-projected need for perfection. You're never matching up to that level of perfection. You're almost in war against yourself all the time.

That is what I feel Katie specifically is working through. This constant battle against herself. And that's a lot to handle as an 18-year-old.

She's also a musician and singer-songwriter. How she responds to that pressure. I think responding with an artistic outlet is something that a lot of artists do. Everybody has to respond in some way.

So for her, it might not be partying; it might not be going out and drinking. Some people like to draw. I think for her, she is drawn to the piano and she's drawn to songwriting, almost as if that's the only way she knows how to communicate: through music.

Interviewer:

What themes do you hope viewers glean from watching *These Stones?*

Katherine:

Some of the themes in *These Stones* I absolutely love—one of them is redemption. There's this hope: "Everyone is redeemable."

No matter where you've been, no matter what you've been through, no matter what you're struggling with. You are seen. And you are loved.

The Lord desires to reach out for you and rescue you and bring you closer to Him. And I love that. I love the theme of hope that is tethered throughout the whole series that, no matter what you're going through, there is hope. I feel like a lot of people in our world have felt like there's no hope left anymore.

It's worth it. Hang on for one more day, one more breath. Take it one day at a time. I also love the theme of, "You are Never Alone." There's always somebody you know. You're not the only one who's going through this, and you're not the only one who's experiencing the pain that you're experiencing.

Interviewer:

How does this relate to the Bible characters brought into modern day times in the show?

Katherine:

A lot of people in my generation specifically say things like, "The Bible is just not relevant anymore. You know, we live in modern times." But the whole point is that, yes, people lived thousands of years ago, but the themes are still relevant even today.

I think a lot of people are going to watch that and say, "Oh, these Bible characters went through the same thing we're going through now."

So I'm hoping they will be able to watch the show, go back into Scripture, read it again, and get to see, "Oh, this applies to me today." I think it'll be really applicable and draw in a lot of different audiences because people from of all ages struggle with the things that are addressed in the show.

BONUS ACTIVATIONS

venture

———•———

Whatever you do in word or deed, do everything in the name of the Lord Jesus, giving thanks through Him to God the Father.

—Colossians 3:17

Aren't we blessed that Jesus set such a great example, being a Man of word and deed? Not only was He a tremendous storyteller and encourager, He backed up His words with actions. We don't want our television series to just be watched as entertainment. Rather, we hope it sparks actions. Starts movements. Especially those that have a ripple effect that help other people.

While the chapters about each episode have *Activations* that you can enjoy as a group or by yourself, to follow are additional *Activations* you can enjoy that are inspired by the series as whole.

Rock Painting

Gather smooth stones, varying sizes, big enough on which to paint a word, a phrase, or a verse. You can purchase rock kits meant for painting or find them in nature. Get acrylic paint supplies in lots of colors, paint pens, and clear acrylic spray.

Before you paint each stone, pray. Pray for the one who will eventually receive it. Ask God what types of encouraging messages should go on the stones.

Next, paint an encouraging word or a Bible reference the finder of this stone can look up. You could even paint a short Bible verse that can fit on the stone and add decorative artwork around it.

Once your words and designs fully dry, use the clear acrylic spray. This will help protect your special message from the outdoor elements.

Just think. *God knows who is going to find these stones!* He knows exactly what message they may need to hear on the day they discover it.

Like Eliana says to McKenna in our first episode, "Look around. You never know when you can be there for someone at exactly the right moment." Even this is a way to do that, to be there for someone with a word they need to hear. Even if you aren't there when they find it.

Once the stones are fully dry, go out in public and find places to "hide" them. I even encourage you to pray through this part too. Ask God to help you find the perfect place to hide the right message for the person who will ultimately come to find it.

The idea is to hide them where people can eventually (and legally) find them. But naturally, not trespass, obstruct pathways, or cause hazards.

Stone Giveaway

Buy a supply of stones that are already engraved with one word or verse on them. Keep a supply on hand. While strangers are likely to find your painted stones in the prior exercise, this is your chance to give a stone to someone when God prompts you to do it.

Be sensitive to His leading for when the time comes to give one away. You never know when that person will be blessed by a Spirit-led message at the perfect time.

Geocaching

For those who've gotten into the sport of geocaching, take engraved stones or ones you create and hide a few of them in geocaches.

Post the GPS coordinates on geocaching sites for others to find. Include a small scroll or guest book for people to sign when they find your treasure.

Often, geocache treasure hunters will take that gift out of the cache and replace it with something they've created for others to discover in the future.

Either way, you've blessed the finder.

THESE STONES Watch Clubs

If you've enjoyed watching *These Stones* alone or as a group, start a new watch club to introduce the show to other people. Consider if you have nonbelievers or seekers in your life who may benefit from seeing the show as well.

For a deeper experience, become a group leader and go through this study guide with them. Take on some of the group *Activations* at the end of each episode or in this segment to do together.

Volunteer Project

Find a volunteer project to get involved with locally. A couple of examples are represented in the show that you can use for inspiration. For example, McKenna works in a thrift store that raises money to help others in the community. Sign up for volunteer shifts in those types of stores, either as a sorter of new materials (like Tanner does for McKenna) or as a front-facing store helper to greet shoppers.

You could also consider a fun shopping day with friends in one of those stores. Especially if you find ones where you know the proceeds directly help those struggling to make ends meet.

Another example is in Episode 1.2 where McKenna and Samuel volunteer to clean up the front yard of a woman who can't keep up with chores while caring for her son with developmental disabilities. There could be opportunities in your community where a single mom or an elderly couple are struggling to keep up with daily tasks.

Take some time to volunteer by yourself or bring a group. Volunteer at your local version of *Circle of Friends*.

Find Your Biblical Courier

Think through an issue you are currently facing in your life. (For example: loss, addiction, sexual sin, temptation.) Research Bible characters who went through something similar in their lives and read their whole story. Write out or talk about how their experiences apply to yours and what actions God may inspire you to take based on these things.

Be Open to Assignments

To borrow a moniker inspired by *These Stones*—be willing to visit "Central Dispatch" through prayer. Ask God who is hurting. While we fictionalize the Bible characters showing up to work undercover today as they are matched to those in need, here's the truth: all of us can be carriers of God's Word a.k.a. Couriers. All of us can be the hands and feet of Jesus to others in a time of need.

A time when they crave to know they are not alone.

Pray about if there is someone struggling in life right now, going through a hard time that could use your presence, your listening ear, and even the wisdom you could share from God's Word about a Bible character who went through similar challenges. But this also can include yourself, your life experience if you've been through something similar.

A New, Yearly Bible

Eliana's practice of getting a new Bible each year was inspired by our playwright and book author's mother, Louise. Tim Stevenson's mother loved to write notes in the margins as she read the Bible fresh each year, recording new insights and applications. Consider getting a new Bible with space to write any insights you have in the margins.

Write significant dates or details about events that prompted the application to your life. Those Bibles with notes will be a treasure trove of wisdom for yourself or your family one day.

Verse on a Mirror

If there is a verse of encouragement that you feel will help keep you on track with your struggles, write it down on an index card and tape it to your bathroom mirror. It can serve as a daily reminder from God Himself.

Blog / Vlog

If you've been inspired to do any of the *Activations* in this book or take an action inspired by the series, *These Stones*, please consider writing a blog or doing a video blog (vlog) to share about your experience. You may encourage others to do the same.

Hashtag the TV show handle #TheseStonesTVSeries so our team can hear or read about it. If you come up with new *Activations* ideas inspired by our show, please share them with us and others.

Create Videos for Family

Eliana leaves behind a series of videos for her daughter, McKenna. They are geared toward parenting, created during those years where they faced challenges together as mother and daughter. Eliana was creating a guide for McKenna's future, on how to raise her own children one day.

Eliana didn't know she was going to die as she made the videos or how important those videos were going to be for McKenna. However, we don't have to be dying to want to leave behind our words of wisdom.

Are there any important messages you want to put on video or in letters to leave for your family no matter when God decides to bring you home?

Capture a Loved One's Legacy

About ten years before my grandmother started showing signs of dementia and memory loss, I interviewed her to capture her life story. I'm so thankful I did, before it was too late. Consider doing this for your loved ones too, no matter how old or young you or your loved ones may be.

Share Your Story

Sometimes, sharing our true story is one of the many ways we and others realize we are not alone. You heard this reminder from me, especially with Episode 1.3. It's not always easy, but it is rewarding to know others can be helped by our honesty.

Is there a story or testimony from your life that you feel ready to share with others for the sake of helping someone else?

You could share your story in person, online, at a speaking engagement, a group, even penning a book. If you are doing this study as a group, consider first sharing your story with those walking through the series with you.

Open Your Heart

(This last one is from Susan.)

Practice opening your heart to new people. You can do this in a variety of social situations, but I'd suggest trying it at church first.

I get it. We all like to catch up with friends we know right after the service. But at least every other week, try deliberately introducing yourself to people you don't know (within the bounds of safety).

You know how awkward it can feel to have no one to talk to in social situations like that—when everyone is chatting it up with friends except you? Open your heart to make that solo person feel seen and welcomed. Keep an eye out for anyone who appears to be alone, downcast, or marginalized in some way.

Be like Jesus to that lonely, disenfranchised, or older person. Remember how the Lord reached out to many that society ignored or rejected (like Zaccheus, the blind, lepers, and the woman at the well)?

Hint: I'll admit that I was a little timid about trying this *Activation* at first. But I learned to push past any shyness and just approach that new person with a warm smile and say, "Hi, I'm Susan. I don't think I've met you before. Are you new here?" Then strike up a conversation from there.

Be the welcoming, open heart of Jesus.

And make a new friend in the process.

Whichever *Activations* you choose to participate in with our growing *These Stones* family, our sincere hope is you are as blessed by them as those you choose to help by your actions. Every stone can be an impactful building block toward hope and healing in someone's life.

The type of moment they will suddenly know:

They are never alone.

And neither are you.

ABOUT THE AUTHORS

CHERYL MCKAY has been professionally writing since 1997. Before creating, then showrunning, and executive producing the multi award-winning *Season One* of *These Stones*, Cheryl wrote the screenplay for *The Ultimate Gift*, which stars James Garner, Brian Dennehy, and Academy Award Nominee Abigail Breslin.

Cheryl co-wrote the faith-based feature films, *Indivisible* and *Extraordinary*, as well as a number of children's projects, including five episodes of the animated series *Superbook* and forty episodes of the audio drama, *The Wild & Wacky Totally True Bible Stories* with Frank Peretti.

In addition to film and television, Cheryl has enjoyed penning novels like *Song of Springhill* and the award-winning *Never the Bride* (with Rene Gutteridge), as well as nonfiction books, including *Finally the Bride: Finding Hope While Waiting, Finally Fearless; Journey from Panic to Peace*, and her three-part devotional series, *25 Dates With God*.

Cheryl's desire from the beginning of her writing career has been to make an impact through words and change the world for good through writing. That's the heart behind serving at the helm of the creative development for Stone Impact Media.

SUSAN ROHRER is a producer, screenwriter, director, and author, specializing in redemptive entertainment and media.

Rohrer's television credits include: an adaptation of *God's Trombones; Another Life* (100 episodes); Emmy winner & Humanitas Prize finalist *Never Say Goodbye;* Emmy nominees *Terrible Things My Mother Told Me* and *The Emancipation of Lizzie Stern; No Earthly Reason;* NAACP Image Award triple nominee *Mother's Day;* the AWRT's Public Service Award winner *Sexual Considerations* (for responsibly addressing the issue of teen sexual harassment); *Sweet Valley High;* TV movies *Book of Days* and *Another Pretty Face;* Emmy nominee & Humanitas Prize finalist *If I Die Before I Wake;* and Film Advisory Board & Christopher Award winner *About Sarah*.

Since 2011, Rohrer has authored numerous inspirational nonfiction books including: her three-book series *The Holy Spirit—Spiritual Gifts; Holy Spirit Whispers, Downsizing, Secrets of the Dry Bones*, and *Kingdom Road*, among others. She is also the author of nine novels in her *Redeeming* fiction series.

Most recently, it was her joy to serve as co-executive producer and director for the entire first season of television series *These Stones*.

—*Soli Deo Gloria*

respond

———◆●◆———

Thanks so much for watching *These Stones* and taking the journey of this *Study Guide* with us. Along the way, we hope you've discovered what a gem you are and a bit more about the living stone God has always meant for you to be.

We'd love to hear about how *Season One* of this television series and this devotional handbook have impacted or even changed your life along the way. If you'd be so kind as to leave a quick review on Amazon, we'll look forward to hearing about your experiences.

Gratefully,
Cheryl, Susan, and the whole *These Stones* team

Made in the USA
Las Vegas, NV
13 September 2024

b2120310-7157-4494-9acf-70198bc57527R01